The Keys *to* My Heart

Melody Alcorn

ISBN 979-8-89130-228-0 (paperback)
ISBN 979-8-89130-229-7 (digital)

Christian Faith Publishing
832 Park Avenue
Meadville, PA 16335
www.christianfaithpublishing.com

Printed in the United States of America

Contents

Introduction

The heart is a fragile thing. It's the easiest to break and the hardest to heal. In the blink of an eye, it can be shattered into a million pieces. Each shard has to be picked up and painstakingly reassembled.

She knew this to be true in theory but never thought it would apply to her. Even though she would say differently, she lived with an innocence and trust that genuinely knew no bounds. The guardrails were low and the rose-colored glasses she wore dark. There was no thought to the possibility of crushed hearts and broken trust. She never factored in the games that everyone played and nobody won. In her world, only happiness and honesty existed; she was unaware of the harsh reality of deception and manipulation.

From her point of view, her heart was safe and would never bear the scars of a love gone awry. She considered her faith to be strong and her identity secure, but she never saw the coming storm that would shake her to the core, prove wrong what she once believed of herself, and cast doubt on what she knew to be true of her Savior.

Within a short matter of time, life changed and then changed again. She scrambled to find her bearings, reestablish her lost identity, and fought to find once more the keys to her heart that she had carelessly handed over.

*****

I'm going to start this off with total transparency. I didn't want to write this book. Sure, I've always dreamed of being an author one day, but what I had in mind was a novel. Maybe a cheesy modern-day Christian romance or a page-turner suspense novel. Possibly historical fiction or a Western love story. This, a book on how to navigate heartbreak, was not in the cards. Life threw me for a loop, and here I am praying that this might help at least one person walking a similar road.

I've struggled with a lot of insecurity in writing this book because, honestly, I don't feel qualified to speak on dealing with breakups and heartaches. A couple of breakups with one being a short, albeit serious, relationship and a few failed talking stages doesn't seem to count as much experience, right? I've come to realize though that the number of relationships, or lack thereof, doesn't really contribute to the actual experience. You can meet someone that you feel like you've known for years, fall head over heels in a matter of weeks, and get your heart crushed within a few short months. The short time frame doesn't make the pain any less real, and it doesn't make your feelings invalid. It sure doesn't take away from the lessons learned.

Trust me, I've been there.

Besides that little insecurity, there was also the fact that I would have to be vulnerable, and for an introverted Enneagram 9 like me who suppresses her feelings, that's pretty terrifying. The Lord can work on the most stubborn, willful hearts though, and before I knew it, I was sitting in a coffee shop in Dallas, Texas, working on the beginnings of a book I had no clue how to write. This book and sharing what I've learned has weighed heavily on me, so much so that I couldn't just ignore it like I had planned. With the encouragement of some trusted people in my life and many sleepless nights that led to this, my dream is now becoming a reality. Just in a slightly different way than I originally thought.

My goal in writing this is to produce a book that I wish would've been available to me while I was stumbling about in the darkest season of my life. My prayer is that this encourages you to take steps to acknowledging, working through, and moving past whatever heartbreak you may have. While this is written from a breakup point of view, I believe some of this can be applied to any painful circumstance, struggle, or disappointment. I also want to acknowledge that this is in no way meant to take the place of any counseling or therapy or, more importantly, the Word of God.

My story may not be the same as yours and I may not know the kind of pain you have, but I do know that we have the same powerful, loving God who can rewrite any story and use it for His glory.

I pray that my story of heartbreak and healing brings hope to you. Through the pages of this book, I'll share some of the hardest moments I walked through and some of the most joyful times since, the lessons I've learned and the regrets I've had, and more importantly, Jesus's love that has become so much more tangible in recent months. And who knows? Maybe I'll throw in a little of the romance I've wanted to write about.

Goodbye Common Sense

It only took one look into his eyes for her to know she was in trouble. It was either going to turn into a relationship that lasted for life or crash and burn. Either way, she liked him too much and knew deep down that she would fall. Not wanting to tumble too fast or too hard, however, she was overly cautious for the first few weeks. She analyzed every word, every action, but all seemed well. There may have been a few potential red flags, but surely she was overreacting?

Each day of spending time with him loosened her resolve. She felt herself slipping with the passing of time, farther and farther, until the few worries she had in the beginning quieted. And then one day, her world slowed as she lost what little control she had of her descent into fully committing to and loving him.

Life had changed in the blink of an eye, and she had no qualms going along with it.

Green Lights

As far as dating, romance, and boyfriends go, I've never been your average girl by today's standards. I had talked to a handful of guys through my teen years but had never gone on a date and didn't really care to date for fun. Nobody I talked to during those years turned my head, and even going into my early twenties, I still hadn't met anyone that I was willing to give a chance. As pathetic as this may sound, I didn't go on a date until I was twenty-two, and let me tell you, it wasn't a great intro into dating. Whatever that was, it ended as fast as it started, and I went right back to trying to enjoy my single life.

At the time, I was working a stressful job, leaving for work early and coming home late, all the while trying to balance it with my personal life, family, and friends. Dating wasn't something I felt I was missing out on. I was just too exhausted and too introverted. My thought was, *If God has someone for me, then He can send him to my job and I can meet him there or He can send him to one of the many people wanting so badly to set me up.* Either way, I wasn't willing to go out "looking" for a boyfriend.

A few months after I turned twenty-three, however, I was settled into a new routine with a new job working from home. My chances of meeting someone at work went from highly probable to concerningly low. Let's face it: If a guy showed up on my doorstep wanting to date me, I would most likely call the police for trespassing. I had to accept the fact that I wasn't getting out at all, and if I ever wanted to meet someone, I was going to have to "put myself out there" (as an introvert, I can't tell you how much I hate that saying).

So I entered the world of online dating.

You may be in one of two camps of online dating. The first camp being you think it's completely normal and fun and all the single people should give it a shot because there are marriages that have come from it, but even if it doesn't end in marriage, it can't hurt. Or you may be in this camp: you hate it. Absolutely despise it. The latter was me, and I refused to sign up. Until I had to come to grips with this being maybe the only way for a selectively social person like myself to have a chance of meeting someone. So I gave it a shot. And guess what? To this day, I'm still not a big fan of online dating. I know a few people who have had success from it, and while someday I may consider attempting it again, at this point I'm neither encouraging or discouraging it. With that being said, please don't take my story as a sign to not sign up for online dating; my word of advice is to approach it with caution.

Now that's out of the way, back to my story…

I went on vacation with my cousin to Disney, and after offhandedly mentioning to her that I was considering online dating, we set up my profile on a dating website. It became more of a joke between us, so I went into it with zero expectations. You can imagine my surprise when a guy halfway across the country messaged me the same night, and I spent time in the long lines for roller coasters that weekend responding to his messages, leaving that vacation with the potential of a new relationship.

I talked to him for about a month, and things actually seemed promising for a little while. There was talk about him coming to visit me, but thankfully we didn't get to that point. I won't spend any more time talking about him because my story doesn't involve our relationship, but let's just say things didn't end well. I wasn't heart-broken at all, but I will admit to some disappointment. I thought us getting to know each other was going well, but it just wasn't meant to be for us. And I was completely okay with that.

After I broke things off with him, I decided to give the dating apps one more go. I signed up for a different app and made sure only guys within driving distance came through as potential matches. I had a few matches and started up conversations with some of them, quickly weeding out the ones where I knew it wasn't going to go anywhere serious (tip for the guys: those one-word responses aren't going to get you anywhere with a girl). Before I knew it, I was down to two guys. I cringe when I say that because I hated the thought of talking to more than one guy at once, even if it's a given on dating apps and even if it was casual; it was overwhelming for me. Both guys seemed great, but I was just waiting for one of them to make a move. Finally, one of them asked to exchange numbers and wanted to take me out, so I told the other guy that I had a date, we wished each other the best, and things ended well between us. You may be thinking, *Why did she tell the second guy that she had a date?* Valid question. Not only did the thought of continuing a conversation with a guy while I planned a date with another not sit well with me, I also found out that both guys lived in the same city. And they were coworkers, although they didn't know it and were in different departments. *Yikes.* That was an honest accident. Even though I didn't tell the second guy who my date was, I wanted to be as upfront as possible just in case our paths crossed later down the road. So I ended that and focused on the guy I did have a date with.

Because of our conflicting schedules, living two hours away from each other, and him getting sick, it was a few weeks before he and I were able to meet in person, so up to that point, our relationship was just through texting. Not even a phone call. It wasn't my smartest move, but because of the other failed talking stage with that first guy from a dating app, I didn't want to get too invested without having met in person. Our only social media connection was through Facebook because he didn't have an Instagram, and I refused to give him my Snapchat. I kept my wits about me in that area just in case he was one of "those guys" on Snapchat. Unfortunately, we all know what I'm talking about. Because neither of us were making a move to have more contact than texting, I had low expectations for our relationship going anywhere.

A few weeks passed, and I woke up the morning of our first date feeling queasy, halfway hoping I'd receive a text saying he still wasn't feeling well and needed to reschedule our date. All the doubts about what I was getting myself into came rushing to the surface, and I almost texted him to say that I needed to cancel because I wasn't feeling well. I turned on my phone and texted him to see if we were still on for that day, and a few minutes later with plans confirmed for a date with a man I'd never met before, much less talked to over the phone, I agonized over my makeup and hair and tried to pick clothes that would be comfortable for an athletic date but not make me look like a bum. Even though I changed my outfit a good ten times, I finished getting ready way before it was time for me to leave, so I just paced and panicked. Why was I doing this to myself?

Going into that first date, I had so many reservations and doubts. Not only was the lack of communication a red flag (on both our parts, really), I had also sworn I would absolutely never date someone with the career he had; too many stories I've heard and relationships I had personally seen not work left me jaded and fearful. But there I was, walking up to meet him and already thinking through an escape plan if the date turned south. It was settled. I would give it two hours to be polite, send my cousin the SOS text, and due to a "family emergency," say my goodbyes to him and make my way home where I could ignore the dating world and lose myself in a good book.

Well, that didn't work.

My cousin stayed on the phone with me to calm my anxiety and keep me from driving away, but eventually I had to hang up when I saw my date walk to me from across the parking lot. I put my phone back in my pocket, wiped my sweaty hands down my leggings, and took a deep breath to fortify myself as he got closer. My anxiety rapidly became worse as thoughts raced in my mind.

Gosh, those profile pictures did not do him justice. This man is really hot.

He's way too good-looking; his personality must be terrible.

I need to get out of here. There's no way this is going to work.

I'm so nervous; I'm going to look like a fool because I won't be able to put together normal sentences.

All of this within the few seconds it took for him to get to where I was.

He was a gentleman and hesitated when he got to me as if he didn't know if he should give me a handshake or a hug (green check mark for him). So what did I do? I went in for a hug. Totally out of my norm for meeting strange men. Great start to keeping my head on straight, huh? We started talking, got our gear for the zipline course, and never stopped talking. I quickly realized I was wrong about my earlier thoughts. His personality wasn't terrible. Not even close. And, what a miracle, I was actually able to carry on a conversation.

It wasn't even five minutes into our date before those plans I had made to escape flew out the window. I had never felt so comfortable around someone I just met, and I knew, although I didn't want to admit it, that my world had just been changed. Those two hours quickly turned into over eight hours as we talked almost nonstop, and his long drive home and the night getting colder were the only factors that kept us from staying out later.

If you were to ask my cousin/best friend what has been the stupidest decision of my life, she will tell you about that date. After grabbing dinner and not wanting the conversation to end, he and I had decided to walk around a nearby park. I know that doesn't justify the lecture and panic I had received from my cousin when I called her after leaving the restaurant to fill her in on our plans. What did necessitate the near-yelling was the fact that it was nighttime, and I was going to be walking in the sketchiest part of town with a complete stranger. Yeah, my levelheadedness was definitely gone. Not the brightest moment I have ever had.

The reason I had gone through with that impossibly dumb park decision was the comfortability and safety I immediately felt with him. Side note: All ended well that evening, and I did make it home with no issue, but still, I won't risk that again. The chemistry between us was undeniable, and we parted ways with the promise that there would be a second date.

Driving home that night, I not only struggled to tamp down the excitement that was building but also combatted the fear that was just below the surface. I hadn't ever felt a connection like that with a guy, and it honestly scared me. Not to mention the career that had always been a deal-breaker for me. I didn't know what the future would bring, but I knew from the first few minutes, I wanted him in it. That longing, along with the unknown of the future, shook me to the core, but I was determined to ignore it and allowed myself to smile like a fool on my way home.

On the second date, I wanted him to meet my parents. I know, I know. That's a big step for a newly dating couple, but I didn't want to get any further in our relationship without my parents meeting him and getting to know him at least a little bit. I trust them both immensely, so their opinion was important to me. I was proud to introduce him to them and vice versa. A week after we met, we went on date number two, I let him come to my house to pick me up, and I introduced him to my parents.

The nerves I felt introducing them to each other almost rivaled the nerves I had meeting him. The awkwardness of bringing a guy home to meet your family is unexplainable. How embarrassing to have to tell your family in so many words, *So this is the guy I'm attracted to, and apparently he's attracted to me too.* Makes me shudder thinking about it. Begging my parents not to embarrass me, I once again paced my house the morning of our date. My dad conveniently had some yard work to do a few minutes before my date came to pick me up, so I rushed outside the moment I saw him walking to the front door, needing to intercept him and my dad. I gave him a hug and felt the "dad judgment" the whole time. My family talked with him for a few minutes, and then we were on our way to enjoy our day together.

After a date even longer than the first, he walked me to my front door, and we had the most awkward goodbye. Giving each other a hug, we both hesitated as we pulled back. Your girl had never been on a second date before then and never had a boyfriend, but I wasn't stupid. I knew very well what the whole *hesitate, break eye contact, and glance at the mouth* move meant. I knew that he wanted to kiss me goodbye. And, *ahem*, I wanted it too. The traitorous side of me wanted to go for it, but the rapidly diminishing, sensible side stopped me. He wasn't my boyfriend, and I wanted to wait until we were official. Add to that there is a security camera on our front porch that my parents can monitor at any time. No thanks. So we left it at that.

We spent the next week after that second date talking through some factors in our lives that could complicate a relationship. We discussed how we weren't "dating for fun" and were instead looking for our future spouses. Talking through a couple of issues such as faith, family (including "our" potential future family), and boundaries in a relationship, I felt we were on the right track. The differences in beliefs were worked through, boundaries were set, and the family topic? Well, we agreed to keep that on the table to continue talking through (more about this later).

He was kind, patient, and I thought he was the sweetest man I had ever met. Making an effort to see me even with the two-hour drive, he made me feel seen and cared for. We clicked, and I couldn't get enough of being with and talking to him. It also didn't hurt that the man was easy on the eyes. The more the time passed, the more comfortable I became, and my mind quieted of any and all warnings.

In my mind, all lights were green and all signs said, "Go."

I won't spend anymore time on the details because I would probably fill up a few pages, but I will give a quick glimpse of what happened over the next couple of weeks. My parents seemed to like him based on that quick meeting and didn't have any major concerns. I went to visit him a couple of weeks later when he popped the, "Will you be my girlfriend?" question. I enthusiastically said yes, and I felt like I was on cloud nine. And, yes, we finally kissed. Far away from any family security cameras.

Over the next few weeks, we fell into somewhat of a routine juggling our work schedules and seeing each other. We hated the long distance, but we were determined to make it work. Everything was looking up, and I was excited to see our story unfold. The excitement and positive signs though still couldn't have prepared me for how fast and how hard I fell for him.

Why Are You Dating?

Our culture places so much emphasis on dating for fun, dating to combat loneliness, and dating just to say you have a boyfriend or girlfriend. The way we date is toxic and harmful. Maybe you can say that dating like this is fine and you don't experience any negative consequences from it, but can you say the same thing about the people you date and the trail of broken hearts you may leave behind? Can you genuinely say that the way you date is leaving people better than you found them?

If we are dating for fun with no strings attached, someone is bound to catch feelings, lose their heart, and subsequently end up with a crap ton of healing to deal with. Dating to combat loneliness is a temporary, Band-Aid fix to a void that cannot be filled by a human, and we will face countless disappointments as the person we're seeking happiness from inevitably fails us. If the reason we're dating is just to please the people around us, make us seem as if we're successful on Instagram to raise those likes, or to elevate our status among peers, then we will learn the difficult way that relationships and marriage are not the be-all and end-all; and the beautiful, serene, blissfully in-love smiles don't show the ugly fights, tears, and sleepless nights behind the scenes. As Jonathan Pokluda, pastor at Harris Creek Baptist Church, has said, "Today's dating is training us for divorce."

Before you even consider dating, determine your motive. Are you ready to settle down and get married in the somewhat near future or are you only trying to pass the time? Do you ache to post an Instagram story of your new boyfriend hugging you or change your Facebook status to say you finally got a girl or are you okay with not being in the same life stage as your friends? Are the lonely nights pushing you to seek outside comfort or are you content spending time with just Jesus and your community even when the struggle to have someone special in your life is real?

Dating with the correct motive may not seem as fun as culture presents it to us, but in the long run, it will help us avoid some heartbreaks. By protecting our own hearts and being respectful of others, the chances rise drastically of us leaving a relationship when needed without the nightmarish ripping of heartstrings.

Online Dating

Even though I'm not on dating apps currently and don't have a ton of experience with it, I do want to share some things that helped me when I did have the apps, what I've learned, and what I would do if I were to sign back up one day.

Online dating is not wrong. I want to start this off by saying that, in our current day and age, online dating is not bad. As time goes on, the stigma behind it is starting to fade as more and more people are meeting their spouses through online dating. Can it be used for wrong purposes and can you meet shady people through it? Absolutely. But you can meet the same kind of people in a church. Just because they go to a church does not automatically mean they are a godly person, and just because they say they believe in Jesus does not mean they are a passionate, converted follower of Jesus. If you personally don't want to give online dating a try, there is nothing wrong with that! But in having that conviction, make sure you don't have the mindset that everyone who does use dating apps is desperate and asking for trouble. You pick your problems in whatever way you date, so what may work for you may not work for the next person.

Be aware that it comes with talking to multiple people. This was a hard pill for me to swallow. I would easily get overwhelmed with having multiple "matches" and would hyper-focus on one guy. If you find committing to one person difficult, focusing on a conversation with just one person at a time is probably your best bet. If, like me, you overcommit, having a couple of *casual* conversations going with different people may help you from getting too involved too fast and getting hurt in the process. However, I would say to cut those conversations off quickly when you don't see it going anywhere significant or when you start dating someone. For example, I knew on the first date with my ex that I wanted to continue dating him. If I had any other conversations going on, even if they were casual, I would have put an end to them. Actually, I took it a little further than that and cut off all other conversations before our first date. I'm not saying that should be the rule, but it is what I felt was most considerate of the guys I was talking with. It's not fair to the person you are dating to continue talking to other people, and it is not setting yourself up well to be able to commit to someone. In a world full of options in every aspect of life, limit those options when it comes to dating to avoid falling into the mindset of dating one person but waiting for a better choice to come along.

Move from online to in-person sooner than later. Like everything, there will be nuances to this. Schedules and distance can all affect this (it was over three weeks before my ex and I were able to meet for the first time), but at the very least, move to phone calls and video chats soon. I made this mistake with my ex, but the guy before him was a little different. We moved from messaging to phone calls and Facetime quickly. You can tell much more from a person's tone of voice and facial expressions than you can a text message. Doing that helped me to see very quickly that a relationship with that first man from the dating apps was not going to work. I know it's intimidating to require a phone call or video chat before the first date, but if they are worth getting to know, then they will happily oblige.

If you're starting to find validation from dating apps, get off. If you're starting to notice yourself waiting around for a message or a new match, give yourself a set time when you check the dating apps instead of constantly looking at your phone for updates. If you're starting to find your self-worth from how many people swipe right on your profile or the sweet words being said to you, it may be time to delete your account. Also, keeping notifications turned off is a big help in not finding validation from the people you're talking with. Something else to consider is if you are swiping right on everyone just to get a potential match. For your own sake and for the sake of whoever you match with, please don't do this. This is a good indicator that you may be lowering your standards and settling for whoever comes along. And please believe me when I say this: Swiping right on every person just to get a match *will* hurt somebody in the long run. Stick around for a few more chapters, and I'll explain what I mean by that.

Going into online dating with a healthy perspective is a game changer. Be aware of the problems that may come with it, keep your standards high in who you swipe right on and who you converse with, and don't let your expectations exceed what is reasonable.

Blindsided

She had never experienced anything like it. All at once, her world came to a standstill and quieted. Like a jolt as if she had been struck by lightning, so profound was the change in her heart. Maybe it was a slow, unnoticeable shift or maybe it truly was a spontaneous change, but either way, it was undeniable. She had fallen in love with him. She knew it with every fiber of her being, yet she still attempted to reason with herself. It was too soon. This was just due to being caught up in the moment.

As the days passed and she continued with her mundane, everyday life, she couldn't ignore what she knew to be true. She rationalized with her brain, but her heart and soul were too entwined. She feared that he would never return the love she had for him and that she would be in this alone. So she waited—waited for any indication that he too had somehow grown to feel the same.

She wasn't left waiting for long. Bliss awaited her in the mirage of his promised waiting arms that caught her as she fell so hard and so deeply into a love she believed was to last.

Cheesy Lines and Roller Coasters

He knew. There was no getting around the fact that he picked up the shift in me. Sometimes, I think I can hide my thoughts and emotions well, but I know for a fact that I didn't do a great job of it that night.

What shift am I talking about? The night I realized I had fallen in love.

For our fifth date, I had invited him over to my place for a homemade dinner and a movie before he left for a work trip. If you were to ask me about any of the movies we had watched while we were together, I could probably tell you the name of the movie, but I honestly can't remember anything about the movies themselves. I think that night we watched a *Star Wars* movie, and to this day, I still have no idea if I liked it or not. What can I say? My mind wasn't on the plot of the movie but on my unfolding story with the handsome man sitting next to me. Yeah, I know, that was too cheesy.

Very early on in the movie, I ended up in his arms and that's where I stayed for the next few hours. We considered watching a second movie but instead spent the rest of our time together talking about anything and everything. We shared our dreams, our childhoods, and random little details that we thought might interest the other. Snuggled up against him, feeling so safe in his arms, we spent a few hours learning more about each other's lives.

And then it hit me with the force of a freight train. I was in love with him.

It was the strangest feeling I had ever experienced. I felt as if I was jolted with the sudden realization, but at the same time, my world quieted and stilled. Words failed me, and my heart went into overdrive while our conversation stumbled to a halt. I attempted to reason with myself. Telling myself I was just caught up in the moment, I tried to believe that there was no way I could have fallen in love with him that soon. That swift fall into love is what you read about in romance novels or see in movies. Surely, that doesn't happen in real life, right? Maybe I didn't even know what being in love felt like and was just imagining things?

Panic started to set in when he noticed the quiet stretching out. I just brushed off his question about me feeling okay and only said that I was getting sleepy from the late hour. Thankfully, since my head was on his chest, he couldn't see the panic that I knew was filling my eyes, and I was able to take a few moments to mentally compose myself. The realization that hit me not only froze my thoughts but also froze me physically. I literally couldn't move. I couldn't talk. I was terrified that he knew my feelings had changed. By the time he left though, I was back to normal. That normal, however, did not include me hugging him a little tighter and kissing him goodbye a little deeper. I thought I was hiding it decently, but there's no way he didn't pick up on those things.

I genuinely thought over the next few days that the "love" that came over me would fade since I was no longer around him and not living in the moment anymore. We had only been dating for less than a month, so I figured it was just an infatuation that I was feeling. I was wrong. The feelings only grew, and I soon came to realize that they were no longer just feelings. I couldn't picture myself without him, and I wanted him with me no matter what happened. The thought of not walking through life with him by my side became unbearable. I knew that the change in my heart was true.

I needed to talk through my mental and emotional calisthenics with somebody, so I texted one of my best friends and asked her to meet me for coffee. She listened patiently as I shared, with quite a few tears, that I had fallen in love with him and was terrified. I was scared that he was never going to feel the same about me. Fear was telling me that I was going to be in this alone and I was going to end up hurt. I was angry with myself and terrified that I had fallen in love with a guy with the career I always said was an absolute deal-breaker. After bouncing all of that off my best friend, I felt more at peace and told myself I would be okay with whatever happened.

Well, telling myself that I would be okay was a flat-out lie as I felt anything but okay late that same night when I went through an intense emotional roller coaster with my boyfriend, and the tentative peace I had found suddenly vanished.

At that time, he was on a work trip for a week and was two hours behind me. Even though I had to wake up at five thirty every morning for work, I would eagerly stay up way too late to spend hours on the phone with him (remembering the days when my phone plan used to be by the minute, I had never been more thankful for unlimited than during that time). That night, as we were texting, I learned about something that he did that I was concerned about, so I questioned him about it. He explained more about the situation in detail, and I justified his actions and decided to believe him, move on, and not let it bother me.

That was my first emotional nosedive of the night.

Just a couple of minutes later, I stared in shock at my phone as the three words I had convinced myself I would never hear from him flashed across the screen. *I love you.* I didn't even care at the time that he had said it over text; I was just elated that he felt the same. The roller coaster of emotions climbed to an all-time high as I told him I had also fallen in love with him.

But it suddenly came crashing down right after that.

There's something about my past that I feel you have a right to know…

Minutes after he sent the above text, he called to drop a bombshell of information on me. My control of my emotions was quickly slipping as I sat in the dark of my house at midnight listening to him share details surrounding a past relationship that could wreck our current relationship. I was completely blindsided. I had already known about some of his past relationships, but not this one because he had purposely left it out in previous conversations. This one was different, changed everything, and added in numerous complications. After almost an hour on the phone together, I told him that I needed to think and pray about what he told me. Reassuring me that he understood my need to process that information and that he would respect whatever decision I made, we hung up, knowing we loved each other but acutely aware that our relationship was left in limbo.

It wouldn't be until months later when I finally recognized the manipulation that I fell right into, and as I'm writing this, only one person in my life knows all the details of that night and how I ignored blatant warning signs. However, the heart is very powerful, and that night, I fell into a toxic habit of justifying his actions.

I may have gotten less than two hours of sleep, spending the long hours crying, praying, and begging God to let this work. I prayed for wisdom in my decision, but truthfully, I had closed hands. Although I asked for direction and even asked my parents for their wisdom (I regret that I purposely left out the more concerning details when I shared with them what had happened), I wasn't going to budge in my decision. I knew what I wanted, and I wanted him. I had fallen so hard for this man and wanted to spend the rest of my life with him. I was going to make it work. Later that morning, I shared my decision with him, and our relationship got back onto the right track.

I remember two nights later walking into my aunt and uncle's house after a brief phone call with my boyfriend. At that point, the declarations of love were still so new and the rockiness between us still too fresh that I wanted to keep it quiet, so very few people knew about what had happened two nights before. Once again, I was proved wrong in thinking I could hide my feelings. Apparently, I was grinning like a fool because both of my guy cousins took one look at the smile on my face as I walked in the house, and while one was pretending to throw up into the trash can, the other rolled his eyes and said, "Oh, gross, she's in love." So much for trying to hide my feelings.

Later that evening, we talked once more for hours. I didn't know it was possible, but I fell in love with him that night a little more. I was all in. And just like that, those few days were the start of another emotional high.

Fast forward a few weeks later, while he was on another work trip, my love was proved for him as I experienced one of the scariest times I have ever gone through. He told me the details of his schedule, so I knew the day his already-risky job would become significantly more dangerous. Because of no communication from him during that day, I thought the worst had happened by the time evening came around. I panicked while one call after another late that night was left unanswered and texts ignored for hours after he was supposed to finish work for the day. Voicemails left saying, "Baby, please just let me know you're alive and okay. I love you," didn't elicit any response. The prayers I was shakenly speaking were a jumbled mess of, "Please, God, don't take him from me. I can't live without him." My thoughts raced as I debated when to get in my car and drive the ten hours to find him. The bright, happy days suddenly turned bleak and dreary as I was briefly faced with the possibility of losing the person I loved the most. That was when I knew with startling clarity just how entangled my heart had become and how deeply I had loved this man.

In case you're wondering, he was fine, and I was immensely relieved and indescribably thankful. But little did I know that later on down the road, I would be praying those same prayers but for a different reason.

Over that time, my love for him became stronger and my commitment to him unbreakable. The longer we stayed together, however, the harder our relationship got. One disappointment after another came my way, but the determination to stay and love him never wavered. In my mind, we were endgame, and I believed he felt the same. Yes, things were pretty difficult between us, and, yes, I cried more often than not, but relationships take work, right? We would make it work. This became my mantra through the months we were together, but I failed to realize that all of this was setting me up for the darkest season of my life.

Red Is My Favorite Color

I don't know about you, but for all of my life, I've heard the most contradictory statements.

I admire your standards for relationships. That's great; don't settle.

But on the flip side, I also heard:

You really need to loosen up some. Stop being so picky and give these guys a chance!

People may have told you to rip up your list, but I'm here to tell you the opposite. Make that list.

I'm not talking about a list of superficial aspects. Tall, dark, and handsome or blond surfer boy; short and brunette, outgoing girl or taller, curvy blonde. Blue-collar or businessman; boss babe in Corporate America or hippie vibes. Rich, somewhat older person or younger rock star wannabe with wanderlust. Forget the car he drives or whether or not she likes the same music and movies as you. None of these will sustain a relationship, and they definitely won't support a marriage. I can guarantee you, all of those will fade with time.

While attraction to some of these more than the other is normal, they should not be the standard.

Instead, make a list of characteristics you need in a spouse. Consider the nonnegotiables. Pray over a list that is Bible-based. You may be thinking, *Well, the Bible doesn't list out dating instructions or exactly what to look for in a husband or wife.* I contend that it does. I'm about to throw quite a few Bible references into this, so I encourage you to spend time studying these and finding more Scripture to support a list of standards in both yourself and a potential spouse.

Check out 1 Timothy 3:2–7 (I realize these are qualifications for overseers in the Church, but if this list applies to them, wouldn't it be wise to apply it to a spouse also?):

> Therefore an overseer must be above reproach, the husband of one wife, sober-minded, self-controlled, respectable, hospitable, able to teach, not a drunkard, not violent but gentle, not quarrelsome, not a lover of money. He must manage his own household well, with all dignity keeping his children submissive, for if someone does not know how to manage his own household, how will he care for God's church? He must not be a recent convert, or he may become puffed up with conceit and fall into condemnation of the devil. Moreover, he must be well thought of by outsiders, so that he may not fall into disgrace, into a snare of the devil. (ESV)

Above reproach/respectable. God's Word translation says "a good reputation." What does his community say about him (Prov. 22:1)? The ideal would be to date someone with whom you share mutual friends. I know this can be taken to the extreme in that some people are known to slander others and spread rumors, so my suggestion is to find trusted people who know both of you. What are his friends like? Does she surround herself with people who influence her to become more like Jesus (1 Cor. 15:33, Prov. 13:20)?

This does not mean to give others complete influence in your dating choices. There were some disagreements from people in my life over my choice in dating my ex because of some superficial aspects about him that they didn't like. I ignored those because those aspects should never be what makes or breaks a relationship; however, one of my biggest regrets is not letting people in on what was really going on between us and what I was seeing in his character. Looking back now, I can see that I could've avoided a lot of heartbreak if I had been honest about our relationship.

So let trusted, godly people in your life speak into your relationships because sometimes they can see things from a different point of view than you can in the moment.

Husband of one wife. Okay, obviously, you aren't going to date someone who is married, so my take on applying this to dating is asking if they are faithful. Is he committed to you and your relationship? Is he committed to his future wife, even if that isn't you, in purity? What is their background as far as past relationships or a previous marriage and how does this affect them today? Does she keep commitments or is she flaky (Luke 16:10)? Does he do what he says he's going to do or do empty promises mark his life (Matt. 5:33–37)?

Sober-minded/not a drunkard. This is kind of straightforward, but I'm getting into it anyway. Does he spend his weekends partying with his friends and getting hammered? Does she have to constantly have a drink in her hand? Is he being influenced by drugs, smoking, or vaping (1 Cor. 6:19–20)? Sometimes, these things may not seem like a big deal, but please believe me when I say that a lack of sobriety is going to cause major problems later down the road down. If not while you're dating, then definitely in marriage. You can't control your actions while under the influence, and that leaves no room for trust. Lack of restraint in these areas is usually accompanied with lying, cheating, recklessness, and so on because the person's judgment is impaired (Eph. 5:18). If these are habits that are not addressed in singleness, you can be sure they will carry into marriage.

Self-controlled. This not only ties into sobriety but also extends to other areas of life (1 Cor. 9:27). Is he pushing you to become physical before marriage? Is he addicted to porn (Matt. 5:28)? Does she get easily angered without a rein on her temper (Prov. 15:18)? Does she have any addictions that she hasn't overcome (1 Cor. 10:13)?

Hospitable. Is the person you're dating hospitable to others, and do they open their lives and homes (Heb. 13:2)? Do they go out of their way to make someone feel welcome in any given setting or are they closed off and are not willing to make friends? Does he freely give of his time to help someone in need? Is she open to sharing resources with others (Rom. 12:13)? Do they treat the person on the street begging for money with the same care they do for someone who is well-off (James 2:1–4)?

Able to teach. The standard with this doesn't have to be that they need to lead a Bible study group or be behind the pulpit every weekend, but does he/she share the Word with the people around them? Are they making a habit of lovingly spreading the Gospel (Mark 16:15)? This can look different for each person as we all have our own spiritual gifts, but pay attention to where their heart is for those who don't know Jesus. On the flip side, find out if the person you are dating is teachable. Does she humbly seek out wisdom and receive correction from the godly people in her life (1 Pet. 5:5)? Is he always searching his heart and actions to see what he can change to better look like Jesus (Rom. 12:2)?

Not violent/gentle. This can also seem clear-cut, but sometimes we can find ourselves in relationships where we can't see abuse, whether emotional or physical, in the moment because of manipulation or, because of our love for the person we're with, we continually give them chances to change. Does he tend to make a point by causing any kind of bodily harm (Prov. 3:31) or does she become harsh with her words (Prov. 15:1)? If there are any tendencies at all toward abuse, please break up with this person and bring trusted community into your situation to move toward healing.

Not quarrelsome. Ask yourself whether he thrives on conflict and always seeks to be right (2 Tim. 2:23–24). Does she have to have the upper hand in arguments? Find someone who will run to conflict to resolve it as quickly and as lovingly as possible (Matt. 18:15–17), not someone who is going to run to conflict just for the sake of a thrilling argument (Matt. 5:9).

Not a lover of money. Is he a workaholic who is obsessed with his next paycheck or does he have a propensity to gamble away hard-earned savings or consistently make unwise impulse buys (1 Tim. 6:6–10)? Is most of her money spent on herself or spent on people she loves and giving to those in need (2 Cor. 9:7)? Is the desire to get rich and live in luxury driving their actions or do they willingly give that up for the sake of promoting God's kingdom?

Able to manage/lead. Are they responsible in work, daily life tasks, and what they own? Can they manage the responsibilities they have or do they constantly procrastinate and make excuses in being diligent (Col. 3:23–24, Prov. 13:4)? Are you dating someone who is a leader and stands up for the truth or someone who follows along with the crowd and succumbs to whatever their friends want them to do (Rom. 12:2)? Being a leader also applies to the man in leading in the relationship. If he doesn't lead spiritually and in purity while dating, he will be equally as passive in marriage. If the person you are dating is unable to lead, they will either be led by someone more convicted than they are (best-case scenario) or led away by those with no convictions (more likely scenario). This isn't a gamble you will want to take.

Not a recent convert. This is a touchy one. If they have only recently come to know Christ, I would recommend not rushing into a relationship but to give it time. Let them fall in love with Jesus completely before they fall in love with you (Matt. 22:37–39). You need to know that they are fully committed to their walk with God, and the ultimate test of this is time. Your priority as well as the priority of the person you're dating should first be a relationship with Jesus (Matt. 6:33). Without this at the center, all other relationships will not last. Make sure the person you are going to marry is running just as hard after God as you; if you're not both running at similar speeds in the same direction, you risk pulling away from each other or from Jesus.

And while you're looking for these characteristics in the person you're dating, make sure your life is displaying the same. No, you will not be perfect and the person you date is not going to be perfect, but I believe these principles are the nonnegotiables. Think of it this way: You are choosing who you will spend the rest of your life with. And while you can make the choice in who your spouse will be, your children will have no choice in who their parents are going to be. I don't say this to cause major anxiety but to caution you to be careful in who you date and give the most important roles to in your life, so pay attention to red flags and steer clear of them. Even if red is your favorite color.

Don't Compromise

It can be so easy to be swept up into the newness of a relationship, the sweet words and flirtatious smiles, and the romance that comes along with it, but, at some point, hard conversations will need to be had. I recommend sooner than later to avoid unnecessary hurt. Every detail doesn't need to be discussed before becoming serious in a relationship, and neither do you have to agree on everything to make it work. There will be some topics you have to agree to disagree on, and that's okay. Just make sure you stand firm in the areas you should not compromise in, and, over time, work through the differences in the topics of lesser importance.

Faith. The most important area to discuss is *faith*. Dating and marrying someone of a different religion is high stakes for divorce, but so is dating and marrying someone who has the same religion but different views on major topics. Start at the basics. Make sure you both agree on the pillars of faith. My rule of thumb is that if it's a differing opinion on a salvation issue, then that's cause for concern, and it would be wise not to move forward. If it's a differing opinion that doesn't impact what you believe about salvation and major theology standpoints, these can be worked through. Personal convictions in gray areas and family traditions are always going to add some complication to a relationship, but, generally, they are not a cause to break up. Combine similar major theological viewpoints with characteristics that prove that the person is running hard after Jesus and you have the potential of an amazing relationship.

Dean Inserra, pastor at City Church, has described faith issues as a theological triage. While he applied this to finding a home church, this can also be used in dating and marriage. The theological triage looks like this:

- First tier: Salvation issue
- Second tier: Church membership issue
- Third tier: Agree to disagree/not a big deal/personal conviction

Salvation issues, or first tier, are nonnegotiables. They are the foundation of your faith, and you and the person you are dating need to be in complete agreement in this area (2 Cor. 6:14). This begins with both being professing Christians and continues into what you believe about the fundamentals of salvation, the divinity of God the Father, Jesus Christ, and the Holy Spirit, and the authority and divine inspiration of the Bible. To quote Pastor Dean, first tier involves *things that are so important that if one of us doesn't agree, then one of us isn't a Christian.*

Another area to tread very carefully in is second tier. This is described as church membership issues, beliefs that do not impact salvation but a difference in belief would be a make-it-or-break-it factor in determining a home church. In applying this to marriage, these would also be essential areas to agree on. Topics that fall into this category would be ones such as views on marriage, politics, parenting styles, gender roles in the home, and lifestyle habits such as drinking limits, financial habits, having close friends of the opposite sex, and family boundaries, just to name a few.

And then third tier, personal convictions, are those gray areas that you can agree to disagree on or even work through with time to come to a compromise. Whether or not you should drink alcohol at all, which church you will attend as a couple if you are part of different congregations, and family traditions and which you will keep or implement as you start your own family unit can all fall under this tier among other topics.

Some of these conversations, like those that fall into the category of salvation issues, should be had early on to determine if it's wise to date. Others may come later on and might be best determined by observing and getting to know each other over time.

Family. Another critical point to agree on is *family*—specifically your future family. This is an area that would trip up my ex and I. Most people who know me know that I love children and have always wanted a big family. I would be willing to have fewer than the six kids I've always wanted (and as I've gotten older, the number has gone down), but even with me caving on the number of children I wanted, there was a slight problem. My ex didn't want kids. At all. We agreed to keep talking about it since he said he could possibly have a change of heart later down the road, but as time went on, I saw that he wasn't going to budge.

The truth is, it's not fair to either of you if one is going to have to cave to what the other person wants as far as a family goes. I would've been miserable if we had gotten married and years down the road he still didn't want children. Likewise, if we did get married and started a family, he might have resented having kids if he didn't truly want them, and our children would've had a father whose heart wasn't fully in it. That being said, the number of kids can be debated; whether or not there will be any kids should not be debated. So find out sooner than later if your desires for a future family align with the desires of the person you're dating. And please don't take that to mean this needs to be discussed on the first date because that's the quickest way to run someone off!

Side note: Ladies, searching for baby shower gifts for friends on his Amazon account (albeit accidentally because you thought you were on your own account) so he could get ads for baby products won't change anything. I may or may not be speaking from personal experience here.

"Oh, hon, by the way, if you start to see baby product ads, that was me. I was looking for a gift."

"Are you trying to get me to change my mind about us having babies?"

"Not intentionally. But is it working?"

"Nope. Kids are just going to tie us down…"

Case in point.

Marriage/divorce. This can tie into both the faith and family topics, but I decided to put this as its own category because it's imperative both people in a relationship agree on their beliefs about marriage and divorce. What do you believe is the purpose for marriage and does this match with what they hold to? What do you both consider as grounds for divorce and is that even an option for either of you?

Marriage is a covenant, not a contract to be easily terminated. It's a beautiful picture of Christ and His bride, the Church, and its goal is to be an earthly reflection of that love. The purpose of marriage is to come together as one in every aspect of life, not to lose your independence, but to combine both lives to become one that is living out kingdom purposes. A husband and wife are to lovingly serve each other and together make disciples for God's kingdom, whether that is through their own children or people outside their household whom they mentor. Like Christ did for His bride, they are to die to their own wants to put their spouse before them. Ultimately, marriage is a partnership built on faith in Jesus and love for each other. Romance and fun should definitely be involved, but this is not the sole reason to come together in marriage. A spouse is a life partner, one with who you walk through life in the mundane days and in the chaotic, painful times. A shoulder you can cry on and a loving heart you call home. Marriage isn't meant to be a smooth, easy ride, but it is meant to be a picture of a unit that sticks together in all seasons of life and a couple that pushes each other closer to Jesus.

If one person in a relationship does not hold to this view of marriage, and I say this as lovingly as possible, get out of the relationship. If either of you have a standpoint that does not reflect marriage as being a sacred gift, then dating is not going to benefit you or the other person, and it will not be a reflection of God's love.

If divorce is a part of either your story or the person you're dating, please have thorough conversations about where you both stand regarding this. What did the previous marriage look like and how does this affect them today? Are there children involved and is the ex-spouse still present in their lives and to what degree? What were the reasons for the divorce, and do they see divorce as another option in their future marriage? If there is a true heart change that now aligns with the correct view of marriage, then I personally would no longer see this as a reason to not move forward. Not everyone will agree with this, and there is nothing wrong with having a past divorce as a personal deal-breaker for a relationship. There will be nuances to this, but what matters the most is that both people in a relationship are living according to God's Word and will enter into marriage with a biblical standpoint where divorce is not an easy way out. Keep in mind to not only avoid holding someone's past against them but also look for evidence of true and continued change in their lives before moving forward.

Life directions. Another important topic to cover is general life direction. What are your hopes and dreams for yourselves five years from now? Is one of you wanting to wait years for marriage and the other wanting to settle down soon? What are your general goals for your lives? If one of you is called to become a missionary overseas and the other is not called to the same goal and instead has a calling that keeps them stateside helping people in their hometown, a relationship may not work. This is not to say that in order to make a marriage work, you both have to be in similar careers or have the same desires and goals in everything. There should be some sacrifice in a relationship, but do make sure the big picture in your callings and dreams are similar.

Connecting the Dots

Something I've had to learn and accept is that there are times when the red flags aren't noticeable. There are some that I ignored, but there were others that were hidden from me. A lot of what I was told ended up being a messy tangle of lies, but thankfully, with time, the truth became clear. It's been said that a person can only hide his/her true character for three months and then it becomes near impossible to keep up the facade.

A friend of mine explained it this way: Sometimes, there are things you see in the person you're dating that don't appear as red flags but little dots. It's not big enough to become this massive, in-your-face warning, but it is enough to make note of. Once those dots add up, you're then able to connect them all and see the true character of this person. And sometimes, connecting those dots can't happen until you remove yourself from the relationship and view them with a different perspective.

If you're like me, you've beat yourself up over missing the warning signs, and I can tell you from experience, this is too big a weight to carry. Yes, I ignored or justified some things but truly didn't see others, and I placed the blame on myself for a long time. For months, I carried shame of not being as discerning as I thought I should be, when in reality, his real character was hidden from me.

It is so important to come to a point where you not only acknowledge where you went wrong in a relationship and learn from the mistakes but also accept the fact that you're not at fault for the way someone else lives their life and has treated you. You are not naive or irresponsible for believing the best in your boyfriend/girlfriend, but giving them the benefit of the doubt has to be balanced with careful discernment.

It basically comes down to this: Hang onto common sense as much as possible, spend time getting to know each other in different environments to find their true character, and seek wise input from the people around you and from the infallible Word of God.

Kiss and Make Up or
Kiss Goodbye?

She wanted to believe him. She truly did. Every part of her heart wanted to take his words at face value. Yet how could she when everything she had been told was false? How could she go to bed at night and sleep peacefully when she didn't know where he was and what was keeping him occupied? She questioned the validity of his every statement, always wondering when the truth would finally make its appearance.

Skepticism eventually replaced trust, giving her no choice but to accept the cold, hard facts. He wasn't who she believed he was. Their relationship was built on nothing but pretense and manipulation. The most jarring truth being that it was all coming to a crashing halt.

She had convinced herself of his innocence for too long. Justifying his actions that spoke for themselves, she had stood by her man. Only, he wasn't her man. Not anymore by the way things appeared.

She had fallen for him, thinking that his arms would be there to receive her, but she slowly came to realize that his arms were nowhere near to catching her as was promised.

Falling Away and Falling Apart

"Honey, if we're going to make this work, I need us to be completely honest with each other. I don't want to have to question everything."

"I completely understand. I'm sorry, babe. This won't happen again."

Those texts were after an early morning phone call when he had, in a roundabout way, fessed up about a lie. Because I was in the middle of a patient's report during work when he called, I was distracted and didn't realize until after we hung up and I finished my report that his call was to cover his tracks and explain that he lied. I was so confused about why he had lied about something that I would have completely understood if he had told me the truth from the start. Without the deception, it would have been a simple situation that I would not have thought twice about. I was upset and hurt, but through the day, I had worked on moving past that and ended up justifying his actions once again.

Even though I had gotten over that and we talked later that day when he called to make sure I wasn't still mad, I had a small, nagging voice in my mind wondering what else he had lied about. I tried to quiet that annoying voice, but it wouldn't be silenced. I started to feel there were pieces I was missing, and it was unsettling. Over the next two weeks, my unease grew as we struggled with our relationship, but because yours truly is an overthinker at baseline and heightened beyond belief when PMS and insomnia are thrown in the mix, I chalked it up to me being too emotional and irrational.

Although I tried to talk myself down from all my overthinking, I knew something was off the day after that phone call. We had plans for him to come see me and join my family for a game night, and because of his long drive and our tendency to stay up too late, I offered for him to stay the night at my place while I stayed with my sisters in my parents' house so that we could spend the next day together also. What I thought was going to be a two-day date got shorter and shorter as one excuse after another came up about why he was so late coming into town and didn't show up at my door until hours after I expected him to be there. Since we were running way behind in getting to family game night, I decided not to bring up the issue. Besides, he was finally with me, right? No need to worry. I could let it slide. So I just kissed him, hopped in the truck to make it to my family event, and tried to move on from my worries. "Kiss and make up" would work better if there was an actual argument to make up for. Just saying.

The quietness between us that weekend, however, concerned me slightly. Once again, I attempted to explain that away. My mind worked overtime to put together the pieces. We both had a very long week, and I was dealing with insomnia, work stress, and pain from a bum shoulder which left me quieter than normal and which may or may not have caused me to doze off during game night. We also stayed up very late that night watching a movie, so in his defense, after spending some time in the sun the next day and asking him to give my bad shoulder a massage, I fell asleep in his arms once again. His week had also been physically exhausting with his work, so I knew he was tired and wouldn't complain about the very chill weekend. I had it all explained to myself. Welcome to how my brain works!

Even with all of that explanation, there was still an uneasy silence between us. Don't get me wrong; I'm an introvert who loves the quiet and loves to spend some quality time in silence also, but there are different types of quiet. There's a comfortable silence where nothing needs to be said, and you can spend time with each other without having to fill the void. It wasn't that kind. This was the silence that was uncomfortable and strained, and I felt like I was walking on very thin ice. It was as if we were standing on the precipice of an all-out fight, and at any moment, we could tumble right off the edge. And that terrified me.

Looking back, I know I should've questioned him and we should've talked more about our little spat about his lie, but my fear of conflict got in the way. I didn't want to fight with him, so I convinced myself that I was reading into things and that it was just an off weekend for us. The following weeks proved otherwise.

The two weeks after that initial lie was just the beginning of the most draining time I have ever experienced. After he had gone home, I immediately noticed a change in him that couldn't be ignored. Initiation from him in any kind of communication slacked off significantly, I was getting blown off more than usual, and there were times when I would be completely ignored. I got over my fear of conflict and attempted to get to the bottom of what we were dealing with, but I was only brushed off.

After a certain situation repeated itself twice in less than a week that left me hurt and pretty angry with him, I tried once more to have a real conversation about our problems. I shared with him that, because of the issues we were having and not knowing what was going on with us, I was terrified of losing him. Those shaky, vulnerable words I had spilled out to him were met with no explanation of the sudden rockiness in our relationship, and I began to slowly realize that these problems we were having could break us. I felt the effort I was putting into us wasn't being returned, and because of some more important information being withheld from me, I was having a difficult time simply trusting him.

Short of dropping in unannounced at his house (and believe me, I would've done that if he didn't go out of town), I tried anything over the next few days to keep us together. By the time the weekend came around, I was exhausted. Mentally exhausted from trying to fit the pieces together of why we were drifting apart. Emotionally exhausted from intense anxiety, fear of the unknown, and deep hurt. Physically exhausted from sleep deprivation and keeping up a front for my family. During that time, I had lived with the pretense of our relationship being uncomplicated, but that happy facade I had displayed collapsed that weekend as I didn't have the strength any longer to keep it up. A simple question from my mom about how he was doing that weekend led to me spilling everything to them, and my parents helped me through my emotional breakdown that day as my fake smiles disappeared to reveal the turmoil I was going through.

Over the weekend, the tension escalated between my boyfriend and I due to a new, very serious situation being added to our already growing list of problems, which turned into well over thirty-six hours of complete silence between us. Those thirty-six-plus hours of no communication were pure misery. I took a step back in initiating contact with him because of my anger over choices of his that were destroying our relationship and also to allow him a chance to be the first to reach out, understanding that he knew me very well and knew the lack of communication was out of character for me. Maybe the way I handled the situation wasn't the best, but it felt like my only option at that time because of the circumstances in which we found ourselves. As hour after hour passed and one day turned into another, I was shown where I stood with him and learned that the place I thought I had in his heart was nonexistent.

The weekend then took a turn when my oldest cousin texted our family group chat to announce she went into labor with her first baby right after the time period of complete silence between my boyfriend and I began. I've never before dealt with the struggle of experiencing two very conflicting emotions at the same time. While my heart was breaking and my world felt as if it was falling apart, I had so much excitement and joy in knowing my cousin was about to meet her daughter for the first time. The day spent at the hospital distracted me from the painful silence between my boyfriend and I, and it made me focus on something other than my problems. My cousin went through a full day of labor and still no baby, so I went home knowing I'd be back the next day for some much-needed baby therapy.

The following day, as I held my cousin's beautiful daughter in my arms, I fought a swell of emotions. Joy for my cousin and her husband. Pride in the amazing parents they would be. Love for this new little blessing joining our family and excitement of seeing her grow up. Exhaustion from keeping a smile on my face while I was actually falling apart inside. Heartbreak because I knew this picture of a loving family would never apply to my boyfriend and I. Unexplainable grief because the hopes and dreams I had of marrying him and holding our own children someday suddenly crumbled to dust as I stood in that hospital room. Heart-wrenching pain as I began to understand that the silence that had just ended minutes before I walked into the hospital that second day was the beginning of the end of us.

The realization that our relationship was not going to survive felt as if someone had sucker punched me. I couldn't bear even the thought of losing him; it made me physically ill. My life was rapidly spinning out of control, and I felt like I was going to buckle under the weight of it all. Even though I knew that it would take a miracle to heal the relationship and repair the damage done, the love I had for him went so deep and the commitment so strong that I still wanted to fight for him. I kept believing for that miracle. I still wanted to hang on tightly to the hope that we would pull through this, so I spent the entire weekend, and especially that last day, begging God over and over, *Please. Please don't take him from me. I can't live life without him.* I didn't know what else to pray. All I knew was that the sentiment echoed the screams of my heart.

Despite me not admitting and believing this for months, God knew what I needed when it came down to what followed after I left that hospital. Not even thirty minutes after I had left, all of our problems came to a head, and because of a lifestyle he was living that was slowly killing the both of us, the man I was going to spend my life with left me with one text message. Had I been given the choice, I would have fought for him, no matter what it took, but that choice was taken from me as his love turned to shockingly cold and lonely detachment.

For him to have walked away without a backward glance, not bothering to fight for us, fight for me, absolutely wrecked me and destroyed my trust. I had given my heart entirely to him, and I feared that if I ever got it back, it would never be whole again.

I wasted so much time after the breakup hoping he would have a change of heart and call or unexpectedly show up at my door wanting to give us another chance. So much willpower was put into not doing those things myself. It had taken over a month to be able to say that I wouldn't take him back if given the chance, yet some traitorous part of me knew that it wasn't true. It took so much more time to fully accept he was never returning. Those desperate prayers I cried out were answered in a way that left me to face the reality of learning to live again without him in my life. I didn't want to believe this was the end. The pain from this heartbreak was so intense that all I longed to do was run from it, and escaping reality as best I could sounded pretty good to me.

The Knot Has Not Been Tied

I'm going to share some information for dating couples that may be obvious and commonsense to some but a lightbulb moment to others, info that I should've taken to heart. *If there is no ring on your finger, you are not committed in the sense you can't break up.*

And to the other camp, I have advice that is also much-needed and that I wish would've been shared with my ex. *Yes, you don't have a ring on your finger, but you are in a committed relationship, so respect the other person until you break up.*

I admit that I overcommitted. I fell head over heels in love with this man and was ready to spend the rest of my life with him. Absolutely nobody else turned my head, and my heart was all his. I was completely devoted to him and assumed, because he claimed to love me in return, that he was as equally committed.

Because of the love I had for him, I justified and ignored warning signs. I explained away the major concerns and red flags that I talked about in the previous chapter that should've given me pause and made me reevaluate our relationship. I think somewhere in the back of my mind, I was believing that because I loved him and thought I would marry him, I couldn't leave him and that I was to continue fighting for us. While all of that commitment is good in dating to a degree, there has to be a line drawn somewhere.

Because when that level of devotion meets his level of disregard, it can only end in indescribable heartbreak.

So how do we balance a reasonable commitment to the person we're dating with wisely ending things when we see major concerns? How do we not become blinded by love and instead see things for what they are and see people for who they are?

This is a question I still ask myself. For so long, I replayed over and over everything from my relationship, and still the question remained. *Where did I go wrong?* I couldn't figure it out. I knew there were a couple of issues with him in the beginning, but they were not deal-breakers for me. They were flaws I was willing to accept because I knew I had my own flaws he had to accept. That man at the beginning was who captured my heart, but the man he really was didn't introduce himself until some time after I lost my heart to him. And I allowed him to keep it even after he proved time and time again that he couldn't hold it with care.

Let me put it this way. If the person he truly was matched with the person he imitated in the beginning and up until the point I fell in love with him, I would probably be engaged to him by now or maybe even married. He would be the one. There would have been no overcommitment. But he wasn't that same person, and he wasn't the one. When I began to see the major issues that didn't line up with who I knew I needed in a spouse, I should've put an end to the relationship. That's where the overcommitment came into play.

If those issues with him and with our relationship didn't exist, the commitment I had to him would have been good and healthy. In a relationship where both are striving to be godly people living for the Lord and working to be the best versions of themselves possible and they are in a good position to be with someone and one day be married, then there are no bounds on the level of commitment. You *should be* all in emotionally, and they *should be* the most important person in your life.

But if one of you is showing signs of commitment issues, it's time to end the relationship. That person is not ready for the step of joining their life with someone else.

What are signs of commitment issues? Most people think of commitment issues as dating around, cheating, and being discontent in staying with the same person. These are all true, but they are just common by-products of an issue that goes much deeper than that. Anything that goes against what was listed in the previous chapter are indicators of a problem with commitment. To put it simply, if they are not committed to God first and foremost, they will not commit to you. It's impossible. When God is at the center of one's life, everything else will fall into place. It will never be perfect, but a healthy, committed relationship is possible because of a perfect God residing as the foundation of both people's lives.

For example, blowing money carelessly indicates they are not ready to commit to support a spouse and future family. They are not able to cherish your heart if they can't respect your body. The safety and security of your relationship is of no importance to them if they are getting drunk every weekend and entertaining people who should remain in their past. It will not be possible for them to love you like they should if they can't love themselves but instead make reckless decisions with their body. If they don't selflessly care for the people already in their lives, why would they be ready to commit to a life of caring for you?

To sum all of that up, if the person you are dating cannot and will not prioritize their walk with Jesus, they will not prioritize you as a boyfriend/girlfriend and definitely not as a spouse. Maybe it seems a little overboard and can come across as harsh, but it will be so much better to determine the character of the person you're dating before a knot is tied that can't be undone.

Grace or Justification?

If it hasn't been obvious, I've had trouble defining the line between showing grace and justifying wrong actions. I've lied to myself and lied to others about the actions of guys I've dated in order to give them the benefit of the doubt. Because I don't know the intentions behind the action or have not seen the full story play out myself, I tend to give a second chance. And another. And then another. All in the name of grace and belief that nobody is perfect.

I've downplayed being stood up multiple times by my own boy-friend, saying that he just wasn't feeling well, when in reality, I knew that there was something more going on behind the scenes. In order to make his character and the way I was being treated appear better than the truth, I would come back into town from visiting him earlier than normal and pretend I was back to help my family with a home project; the fact being that the man who claimed to miss me sent me home because he couldn't prioritize his girlfriend he hadn't seen in weeks over a video game with friends. I've let myself be treated as last choice to allow for leniency in schedules and mental health, only to come to the harsh realization that these were nothing but excuses and a ploy to manipulate my emotions. Wearing blinders that concealed major lifestyle and character issues plain as day, I would talk up his better qualities in a futile effort to convince others and myself that the person I fell in love with was who he really was. In an attempt to continue extending grace and choosing to love despite it all, I remained in a state of denial when the man I thought I knew peeled the mask away to reveal a man I didn't know.

For a long time following the breakup, I thought it was the concepts of grace and sacrificial love that were slowly killing me. But it was only blinding justification. While I did love him to a degree that I don't think he fully understood and in a way he never actually reciprocated, that love was fatal to us both. It held us in a place that was no longer healthy. It entrapped me in a lie that he loved me in return and our relationship would survive, and it promoted a lifestyle he was living and ways he was treating me with no fallout.

This whole time, I thought I was showing grace, but truthfully, I didn't understand what grace actually meant. I had to go to the Word of God to find out what His grace means for us and how that looks for His children to be an extension of that grace.

Grace, according to Strong's Concordance entry G5485, means unmerited favor, goodwill, and loving-kindness. Ephesians 2:8 tells us that we are saved by the grace of God. It is not something we have earned; it is a gift. When we are saved by His grace, this means we are accepting His forgiveness of our sins. Through grace, He canceled the punishment of our sins. Our lives as Christians revolve around the freely given gift of forgiveness offered to us by Jesus, and out of that forgiveness, we should extend it to others. Ephesians 4:32 says, "be kind to one another, tenderhearted, *forgiving* one another, as God in Christ *forgave* you" (emphasis added). The word for *forgiving* and *forgave* is linked to G5483 in Strong's. And guess what? This word is very similar to the meaning of grace. It means to show one's self gracious, kind, benevolent, and to show favor.

So if I'm tracking with this correctly, to extend grace is to extend forgiveness. I think we tend to apply a false meaning to grace, making it out to be a heart posture that accepts wrongdoing, withholds true forgiveness, and moves forward without making necessary changes to boundaries. Instead, it should be a heart posture of understanding that, yes, nobody is perfect but also not justifying sin. Grace does not mean to accept or make excuses for the hurtful actions of others. What it does mean is to forgive as Christ forgave us, yet forgiveness does not always mean restoration or continuation of a relationship (more on this later).

Grace *does not* mean keeping someone in your life and allowing them to have your heart when it's clear they do not value it. Grace *does not* mean making excuses for the ways they repeatedly hurt you. And while grace may merit a second chance, it *does not* mean continuing to give wasted chances.

Sometimes, because of our love for someone, we have to let them go. If our love enables wrong actions and promotes a lifestyle that just harms both people, it might be time to say goodbye. For a lack of better words, this absolutely sucks. The pain will be terrible, and it will be one of the hardest choices you have to make. But sometimes, kissing and making up will just prolong the misery and hide deep issues that are best resolved by leaving. Sometimes, it's best to let that last kiss be a kiss goodbye and allow yourself and the other person to find true identity in Jesus and press closer to Him.

Press Closer to God

She felt the cold, sharp knife of his actions slice her heart. The wound was left painfully exposed to the elements as he abruptly ripped the knife out when he walked away. Attempting to cover the wound with a quick fix or ignoring the pain altogether were useless for it would only rip open once again and leave her gasping for air, shaking from the intensity of the pain. She was drowning in a deep and murky ocean of heartache and dejection; every mention and remembrance of what she lost was comparable to saltwater being poured onto that open wound, forever reminding her of its sting.

Why call it a flight or fight response when both actions are in use? She ran as hard as she could from the pain, from the loved ones who were supporting her, and sadly, from her God who loved her and was ultimately in control. Simultaneously, she fought against Him, refusing to believe that this was the end and angry that He allowed the plot of their story take a turn for the worst.

Escaping Reality

My heart shattered as I read the text saying that we were over. I felt like he had ripped my heart out, stomped on it until it was in a million pieces, and then handed it back, literally saying, *Best of luck to you*. I had never felt pain like that before, and I was paralyzed. I didn't know what to think, didn't know what to say. In the days following the breakup, I had thought of many more responses to that text that I could've used, but at that time, I was so very lost. When that text came through, I was curled up into a ball in the driver's seat of my car at a parking lot, bawling to my mom on the phone and typing out a return text of the only words my brain could formulate. "That's freakin' it? I was a fool to believe you actually loved me."

Through broken sentences and harsh sobs, I gave my mom the rundown of what had happened. The words she said will forever stick with me.

"Baby girl, you need to press closer to God in this."

I don't remember saying anything in response to that, but I do remember thinking that taking that advice was the last thing I wanted to do. The man I loved just dumped me, and I thought I was going to have to open my car door to hurl onto the parking lot of the nail salon I was at. All I wanted was to go home and lock the world and everyone out, including God. So yeah, my stubborn, heartbroken, and bitter self rejected her words.

My life had just been turned on its head. All the hopes and dreams we had together suddenly vanished with the tap of a screen. The panicked fight and effort I had devoted in a desperate attempt to keep the dry-rotted walls of a doomed relationship from collapsing were for nothing. The man who had quickly become my world and stolen my heart strode out the door and left an emotional hell behind him for me to endure without sufficient explanation or any care for the pieces of a heart I foolishly thought he cherished. I was deceived repeatedly by who I thought was completely trustworthy, abandoned by the one who claimed to love me, betrayed by a man I had shared the deepest parts of my heart with, and oh-so alone. *Press closer to God?* How? Where was He in all of this?

The chaos inside my mind was frightening. Newly exposed facts and imagined scenarios chased each other around in a blurry whirlwind. Behind my pain-glazed eyes, there played a movie of my life over the previous few months, a dramatized mystery that gave no clues as to what was legitimate and what was an act. I was haunted by the continuous echo of the question, "Was any of it real?" Fear of the future waltzed in the door of my mind and dropped its baggage as if to stay, and the cost of betrayal draped heavily over me like a cloak. The light shut off inside me as if the power was cut and turned the tumult into a dark void. He was gone, and so was I. Trapped in what felt like a fever dream, I wondered when I would wake up to find this all to be only a nightmare and see that we were both still present. My head spun with this inner turmoil, and my world seemed to come to a standstill while life outside continued without slowing down.

The amount of willpower I put into appearing semi-normal around people was insane. I would mentally compartmentalize my thoughts and refuse to think about him or the pain constantly coursing through me during family days on the lake and at the pool or girls' day out for brunch so I could be present with my family. I utilized that mute button on Microsoft Teams frequently to take deep, calming breaths and clear the tears from my voice when I was asked to give training sessions at work starting the day after my world turned on its head. When I was around other people, bathrooms became my refuge so that I could let the mask fall momentarily and scramble for a mental grip once again. But in the too quiet solitude of my house where I had nobody to distract me and no pressure to keep a somewhat normal appearance, I had to either face life or numb out. I chose to numb out.

Everyone has a way to deaden the pain and forget the present. Mine was losing myself in work and binge-watching TV. I had started doing that the week before we broke up due to the unresolved problems in our relationship. During the day, I'd work myself into exhaustion while solely on autopilot; so much so that at the present, I can't remember anything work-related from those months because of how out of it I was. I'm honestly surprised that I passed my audit for that quarter. In the evenings, I'd watch a few (okay, more than a few) episodes of a TV show. Nights were especially rough, so I would stay awake until past 3:00 a.m. trying to escape my crappy reality by watching a made-up reality (for the Marvel fans, *Agents of S.H.I.E.L.D.* is a pretty great show; I just don't recommend watching four seasons of over twenty episodes each in less than two weeks).

The pain from my shattered heart drove a burning need to be completely alone. I'm quiet and introverted to begin with and need alone time on a regular basis just to function in society, but this was more than that. The misery I was in beckoned me to jump headfirst into a sea of isolation, and I was standing on the diving board, peering over the edge and longing to lose myself in the depths of complete solitude and just float along the waves of self-pity and heartache. The desire to enter into total seclusion was not so I could face the facts and process my grief but to wade in the bittersweet memories and avoid anything and anyone who may push me to take steps toward healing and letting him go. So to numb out by myself was appealing.

I wanted to run. Not physically run (please, that's against my religion). But run away from life. From reality. From the pain that haunted me and threatened to pull me to a place of no return. I wanted to deaden the ache and forget all the wrong going on in life. I just wanted to get away because everything reminded me of him. So I opened up my Airbnb app and booked a weekend trip to the beach. I know, rebellious. But I paid way too much for it because it was in-season at a touristy beach, so that counts for something, right? I started to pack my bags and put in a request to my boss to take half of that Friday off to get to the beach a bit earlier. And then I felt a nudge to do something that was going against the lure to the darkness of that self-imposed exile: Invite someone to come with me. I wasn't going to tell anyone I was leaving for a solo tip until maybe that Thursday night, possibly Friday morning, so this threw a wrench in my plans. I called my cousin/best friend and told her of my spontaneous trip and asked if she would want to come. Before I knew it, I had also asked my brother to join, and what was supposed to be a weekend of hiding away in my condo all alone to wallow in the pain became a sibling/cousin bonding weekend.

I wasn't upset at all about the change in plans, but in the back of my mind, I was secretly planning to make that solo trip back as soon as possible because I thought I needed it. Let me tell you, I was so wrong. Taking a solo trip would've been a terrible mistake at that time in my life when I refused to confront the pain and grief head-on and instead numbed myself to my thoughts and emotions. A mistake I realized the first day of vacation.

Unbeknownst to my cousin and brother, regret in the beach town I chose to get away to slammed into me with the force of a semitruck the minute we crossed into Okaloosa County lines. I don't know how, but in all the craziness and upheaval in my life, I had managed to forget that my ex and I had been planning to go to Destin when our lives slowed down. This was supposed to be our getaway. It started as a joke to escape the social events we had on our calendars and dreaded attending, but the joke became more alluring the more we talked about it. Because of our mutual love for Destin, we decided to actually make that a reality as soon as we could. And here I was, driving over the 331 Bridge, attempting to get away from memories of him but only cruising right into another unfulfilled dream we had. I saw signs to places he had wanted to take me and glimpsed the parts of that city I had grown up visiting that I was going to share with him. Attempting to relax on the shoreline of the Emerald Coast only twisted the knife in my heart as I saw couples walking hand in hand, a picture of what I thought we should've been. I had run to Destin to escape and be alone, but suddenly, I wanted to run right back out, far away from the continuous haunting of broken promises and dreams.

Although distraction isn't typically healthy, it was much needed that weekend. Looking back now, I can't imagine how I would've handled the sudden assault of pain that had overtaken me that weekend without my cousin and brother there to distract me. Talking about it would've been helpful, but I didn't know how to, and the times I had attempted to share what was on my heart with the person I loved the most had failed miserably. So, in my mind, there was no point to it, and frankly, I was scared to talk about the frightening pain that had overtaken me. The next best thing was to not be alone even if that wasn't what I was craving at the time. Still, I was avoiding the hard work of sorting through the chaos inside my mind and the hurts piling up in my heart.

My attempts to run from everyone around me, hide from reality, and ignore the hurt backfired each time. With each escape, I returned emptier and alone. The wounds I tried to cover up reappeared with every reminder of what I had lost. Trying to forget what happened was useless. Small triggers would set me off and leave me overwhelmingly burdened with the weight of grief. Reality was knocking on the door of my heart, and there I was, hiding in the corner with the lights off, pretending nobody was home.

Before too long, I couldn't take it anymore. Sure, I had prayed a little bit here and there, mainly short phrases like, *God, please help me*, but actually opening up to God about how I really felt? Nope. I couldn't do it. Anger for what He took away clouded my mind, and distrust prevented me from reaching out to Him. This condition I found myself in only further bogged me down. But then I reached the end of myself. I couldn't carry the weight of the pain. My head was spinning from the roller coaster of suppressed emotions, and I was exhausted from the sudden fall into depression and loneliness. I wasn't strong enough to handle it all on my own, so I finally broke down and let it all out.

I sat on my couch one Friday night with a glass of wine, and on the Notes app on my phone, I started to type out what I was feeling. It started as just an outlet for me and was only going to be a couple of paragraphs long, but once I got going and realized I was actually processing everything, I couldn't stop typing. Somewhere between a diary entry and a prayer, I wrote it all down in a journal a few days later, and it ended up being six pages long. It was a mess and barely legible, but it was honest and real. From that point on, I was journaling and writing in my prayer journal almost every day. It was so hard to get my feelings out to God, but it was the best thing I could have done because I soon began to see a gradual difference in myself. It was a two-steps-forward, one-step-back kind of progress, but it *was* improvement even if it was slow.

The weight from all of my hurt, frustrations, anger, and distrust left me with no choice but to decide between two options moving forward. I could either let it utterly consume me until I became a person I no longer knew or lay it at the feet of Jesus. I couldn't do both. I tried both ways, but the only option that brought some semblance of peace and comfort was the latter. Carrying the pain myself and refusing to allow healing to take place would only cause bitterness to take root and turn my heart to ice. But there was a better option. Harder, yes, but worth it. I could let the Healer and Comforter of my soul shoulder the burden and thaw the chill starting to take over, ultimately allowing Him to bring more growth and freedom over the coming months than anything I could ever imagine.

Running Scared

Have you ever driven your car when you knew you weren't supposed to be driving it? Like when your dashboard is lit up and there's some weird rattling noise coming from the hood, so you just put on your darkest sunglasses to dim the glare from the warnings blinding you from the dash and blast your radio to conceal the sudden out-of-tune symphony playing from the engine. You know you should take it to the mechanic as there is obviously an issue that needs to be addressed, but you put it off for as long as possible and make all kinds of excuses. *I don't have time to bring it to the shop…Everybody is so busy; I don't want to bother anyone by asking them to pick me up from the mechanic…It's going to be too hard to come up with the money for the repairs…I really don't know what the mechanic is talking about when he tells me what's wrong with the car; it's too confusing…*

How about when we have physical pain but we try to minimize it? Remember that bad shoulder I mentioned in the last chapter? I made every excuse in the book to not see my doctor about it for a year. I didn't have decent insurance that would cover the doctor visit or imaging, and out-of-pocket expenses are outrageous. I also didn't want to have to use my PTO and make time in my schedule. But the real reason was because I was scared. I was worried about what they would find and that the healing was going to be too painful and too complex. I didn't want to face the possibility of surgery and that terrible recovery. So I put it off and just attempted to cover up the pain with ice packs, the occasional use of a sling, and Extra-Strength Tylenol for when the pain was intense. I would be in tears from the agony but refused to get to the root of the issue. It had to take my ex-boyfriend seeing me constantly uncomfortable and him telling me, "Make an appointment with your doctor now," for me to finally seek help. Honestly, I really only made that appointment so I wouldn't seem like a crybaby to him about going to the doctor. With much dread and fear, I saw my doctor and got imaging done. Thankfully, the issue didn't require surgery, but I was able to learn what to do for it and make adjustments to correct the actual problem and not just the symptoms.

Don't we tend to similarly rationalize our ways of coping with emotional trauma and pain as we do with the way we ignore the problems with our vehicles? Because it's too confusing to confront or too difficult to handle, we push it to the side. Isn't the way we attempt to temporarily fill the void in us kind of like the way we treat the symptoms over the root issue? We pull through the emotional breakdowns, ignore the deeper problem, and implement avoidance strategies only to start this nonstop cycle anew. We find ways to cope, but in doing this, we only exacerbate the underlying problem and prolong healing, and we do this because we buy into the lie that the healing process will be more painful than our current situation.

Our natural response in times of pain is to run to anything that may dull it. Some chase the party scene and hookup culture. Others closet themselves in their house and drown the pain by overworking (and all the introverts said, "Amen"). Alcohol, drugs, stress-eating, affirmation from social media, or anything that is the sole focus of our time and energy to ignore the present and numb the pain are typical coping responses. All of these, no matter how severe the coping mechanism, are just quick fixes to a deeper issue. The more we turn to these sources to ease the ache in us, the bigger the hole in our heart becomes, but the sooner we face our problems head-on, the cleaner the healing will be.

Like my fears with my shoulder problem, I think we tend to become scared of confronting the pain we live with. If we were to face the pain instead of running from it, what other unrealized hurts and wounds might come up that only add to the trauma? What flaws about ourselves might be revealed? What if we ran to God with our anguish only for us to be cut open further?

Facing what is hurting us and digging through the rubble to find the neglected wounds is difficult. It takes time and effort, but in the end, it's worth all of the work because those wounds will finally be tended to and properly patched up. In allowing our pride to be bruised and exposing our own mistakes and character flaws, we open ourselves up to uncharted growth and increasing potential to become more of who God calls us to be. Sometimes, surgery is necessary to correct an internal issue. It's painful and the recovery is slow, but if there is an unseen problem, we have to allow the Surgeon to cut our hearts open to remove what is dying inside and repair the damage.

It's hard to put an end to what we use to cope with the pain, and it can feel awful to stop running and face the hurt. The easy way would be to continue to avoid anything deeper than surface level and just dull the ache with temporary fixes, but these ultimately become the more difficult road to walk. At some point, we have to come to the end of ourselves and allow God to heal and comfort as only He can do.

Hard Stop to Insanity

I'm a big country music fan (please don't judge me for that), and we all know that there are quite a few country songs that are about heartbreak. Lyrics such as: "I used to be your 6 a.m. 'Hey, good mornin', beautiful. How ya been?' I used to be a 'we just landed; miss you, can't stand it. See you this weekend'" in "Lonely Call" by Raelynn reminded of what I used to hear from my ex word for word. Morgan Wallen's "I've been working hard to fade your memory, baby, but the only thing faded is me. I need something you-proof" did not help the seemingly impossible concept of moving on from him. Over and over, these songs and many others played on my Spotify playlist. The tears that were already coming way too easily and frequently would become an onslaught when those heartbreak songs played. Not to mention the love songs that used to play when I was with him pushed me even further into misery whenever a shuffle of my playlist would repeat those lyrics previously sung to me.

I'm also a sucker for a good rom-com, but those also didn't help my state of mind. Some movies were worse for me to watch than others. One new movie on Netflix with a storyline that had similar elements to a situation with my ex left me an emotional wreck not even twenty minutes after pressing play. I remember telling two of my cousins about the movie, and both looked at me like I had lost my mind. "Why would you watch that one?" It was a terrible decision that only caused me to dwell on the pain even more. Even though it was just a movie, I was not in a healthy place and was unable to take in any entertainment that was providing unnecessary reminders of what I was going through. My focus should've been on my relationship with Jesus; instead, I was zeroed in on movies, music, and social media that were pulling me away.

For my own sanity, I had to put a stop to it.

When I began to see the trends in the emotional breakdowns, I knew it had to do with what I was feeding my heart. For over a month, I gave myself strict restrictions to social media and entertainment. TikTok was completely off-limits unless it was a direct message from family. Instagram and Facebook were limited to only one to two minutes a day at most as I would only view posts from family and very close friends. I canceled Netflix and stayed away from Disney+, only allowing myself to watch a movie or TV show if it was a family night. My Spotify changed from country and rock genres to strictly worship music, and the novels on my bookshelves collected dust as they weren't touched for what seemed like ages.

After the month ended, I found that I wasn't as excited as I thought I would be to allow myself access to more entertainment. Binging shows no longer held any appeal, and it was over six months before I picked up a novel. I was able to implement better habits of listening to worship music first in the mornings before I let myself switch the playlists up to rock or country. My emotions slowly started to come back under control after I stopped allowing outside influences to manipulate them.

It may seem overboard, but sometimes you have to go to the extreme because you are on the polar opposite end and need to balance yourself back out. This can look like taking a month-long fast like I did or it can be a permanent hard stop. Only you can determine what is healthy for your state of mind with the input from people who know you well. Surround yourself with accountability to keep yourself from feeding your heart things that are preventing your growth.

I Am Not Alone

I'm going to share something I've only admitted to one person. It's seems so silly now, but I'm not proud of it because it shows just how desperate I became and how broken I was. In a time of grief and loneliness, this seemed to be what would help in the moment. However, it was anything but helpful.

One month after I had deleted and threw away any trace of my ex-boyfriend that was left behind, loneliness struck me harder than normal one night. That day had gone well. I was doing okay emotionally (I say *okay* lightly), and I had taken some positive steps toward healing. But all of a sudden, when I was alone in my house that evening once again and facing yet another night of the ongoing, nightmarish insomnia I was fighting, the loneliness that was constantly lurking around me rushed in full force. Missing the man I had loved—and probably still did love at that point in time—left me with an irresistible need to see him and to know how he was doing. What I wanted most was to talk to him, but since that was impossible, reminiscing with old pictures would have to do. Then I realized I had nothing.

With an almost frenzied response to this, I tried to decide what I should do. I no longer had his number, so I couldn't call. I deleted every picture and video I had of him. I was much too ashamed of this relapse and way to full of pride to ask my mom to text me the two pictures she had of us that I had sent her months earlier. Needing to see his face so badly, I pulled out my phone to scour the internet for any evidence of him. I wasn't trying to be that crazy ex-girlfriend who had to know what he was doing just to add more evidence of wrong to the list to seethe over or seeing our lives as some sort of competition. I just simply missed him.

The most obvious answer would be to look up his Facebook or Instagram, but since he no longer had either, that wasn't an option. But I checked anyway to see if he reactivated his account. Facebook. Instagram. Spotify. Yeah, I got desperate enough to check music streaming platforms. Nothing. I'll admit to being even crazier and trying to find his family's socials to see if there were any posts about how he was. Nothing. I admire people who aren't pulled into the lure of social media, but this was ridiculous.

So I googled him. Pages and pages of search results made for so much time spent in trying to find a picture or some information on what he was now up to in life. I can't remember how long I spent combing through internet archives, but I finally found a hit. I stumbled upon two pictures of him as a senior in high school. Although it was from years ago and he had looked different when I knew him from when he was a graduating senior, it was still him. It was still that same face I was missing terribly that night. And seeing him again, albeit in pictures from years prior, broke me even more than I already was.

Thinking that finding some new information about him or seeing a picture of the man who had crushed my heart would bring some closure by reminding me that I was better off without him, it had the complete opposite effect on me. My heart stopped and then raced forward at a painful speed, causing sharp pains to slice through my chest. I couldn't breathe because the picture I was looking at was just a cruel reminder that he was no longer in my life and that I was by myself. My stomach churned with the nausea from the physical manifestation of emotional trauma. I stared at those pictures for what seemed an eternity, sobbing from the renewed pain, struggling to breathe against the overwhelming loneliness caused from being apart from him. He was no longer a phone call away, and there was no longer a promise to look forward to of seeing him after a long absence. I felt completely alone, and despair was creeping in my heart. This was one of the many panic attacks I had begun to experience that year.

I sat for what felt like hours and struggled to find some mental grip. I was physically shaking and unable to breathe. Stuck in a pit of panic with no light, I stumbled and fell continuously, trying to find a handhold to climb out, but there was nothing but smooth walls and terrifying darkness. The reverberations of a falsehood that told me I was entirely alone with not a soul to guide me through bounced off the interior of the abyss and were absorbed by my mind. Oxygen felt as if it was rapidly diminishing only to be replaced by the dank, foul wind of fear. How did I get here and why couldn't I climb out? The loneliness wasn't new for me, but since removing the avoidance strategies from my life, this was the first time I had to face the music with nowhere to run for an escape.

With no beach town to flee to or Netflix show to zone out with, my only option was to pray. It sounds cliché, but that was literally all that was left for me to do. I don't remember what I prayed or how long I sat there pouring my heart out to God. I do remember somewhere in the back of my mind being thankful that He could understand what I was saying because not a word was making sense to me. All I know is that the panic, fear, and overwhelming sense of loneliness slowly shifted midway through my prayer to a serene calm, assurance that I wasn't actually alone, and an astounding sense of peace. It didn't erase all of the feelings, but it slowly replaced some of them and introduced a new stillness that allowed me to finally breathe again.

When someone becomes such a crucial part of your life, the absence of that person can feel like a part of you was violently ripped away. The loneliness that follows is oppressive and strangling. You have days where you think you're moving on in life, but in the hush of solitude with the dark pressing in from all sides, loneliness strikes with a vengeance.

Loneliness is real and valid, but it is not defining. Just as physical symptoms alert us to an illness and push us to seek a cure from a doctor, so those forlorn feelings drive us to pursue Someone who will bring light to that darkness. They are the nudge to send us running into the arms of One who will never leave us. Does this take away the ache to physically feel the arms of the person you miss holding you or their gentle voice soothing you? No, it doesn't. That ache can still linger, but it is no longer controlling. Peace that can be found nowhere else fills that pit and lifts you out as light invades the shadows and guides your way.

Even though I strongly felt like I needed the comforting embrace of my old boyfriend around me once more to chase away the emptiness or his deep voice to calm me and pull me back to reality, I found that these were only phantom pains that pushed me to find the true source of comfort. I longed to be seen and known once more, so I ran to the only One who fully sees and knows me and still loves me even in my lowest of lows.

In the darkest moments, when Jesus is all you have, you realize that Jesus is all you will ever need. That's when the irrefutable truth sinks into the weary soul: You are never alone.

52

Addicted to Love

Loving him was an addiction. Seeing his smile and hearing his laugh fed the dependence. Each kiss and touch rooted in her soul, and every shared look and word spoken embedded in her mind. She was on a high loving him and didn't know until she crashed.

As if experiencing withdrawals, she yearned for the sound of his voice for weeks to come. She would lie awake in the dark, wondering if he felt even a fraction of the pain that was searing through her. She would sob into her pillow as her heart screamed at her to make one phone call. Tortuous thoughts would give way to tortuous dreams once she would finally drift off at 3:00 a.m. Images of his face would flit through her mind, so vivid but not close enough to grasp. As if awakening from a drunken stupor, she would drag herself from her bed to continue life, always aching to send one text. Just one call to see if what was done could be reversed. One more shot at the dream to which she once clung.

Loving him and giving him another chance beckoned to her, and she longed to heed its call. She lost her lover and best friend and felt as though she was drowning in the pain, but he was an addiction she was determined to overcome.

Happily Never After

Can I share a hot take with you? I hate Siri. I guess it's helpful when you need to be hands-free for a task and you want to call someone or when you need some random information from the internet. But let me tell you, Siri needs to keep its suggestions to itself and mind its own business.

I hear you. You're probably thinking, *Wow, her boyfriend dumped her and she's taking it out on a robot. She might want to talk to a therapist about this one.* Let me explain a little more about how Siri made me want to throw my phone in the fire pit outside my house, toss in a match, watch it light up, and forget technology.

I can't remember exactly how long it was after the breakup, but one evening, as I was about to turn off my phone for the night, I accidentally swiped down on my home screen and Siri suggestions revealed itself. I couldn't imagine a worse first suggestion. Siri thought it would be a great idea if I were to send my ex, "Goodnight, babe. I love you." Insert red hearts and kissing emojis. Siri already had it typed up and ready to go as if that would make my evening so much easier. One tap and I could send it. Just one touch and I could cave to the longing that had been eating at me since that dreadful Monday afternoon when my world came crashing down around me. And it made not contacting him seem impossible.

Like an addiction, I had to constantly fight the temptation to text or call him to try to fix what was broken. If something happened in my life, my first instinct was to pull out my phone and tell him. Like the day my cousin had her baby and I wanted to send him a picture or when I wanted to tell him some of the amusing things my siblings did when I kept them for a weekend. It was so difficult to not call him to get his opinion on decisions I needed to make or to share about my day when life was hard. I fought against the pull to contact him during two more of his work trips that I knew were scheduled after the breakup because I wanted to make sure he got there and back safely. There were countless times when a situation or something I had seen almost caused me to call him up so I could make him laugh, and there were instances when I had the thought, *I'm going to buy this for him because he would love it…Oh wait, never mind.* I very nearly succumbed on multiple occasions to the desire to get in my car and drive to his house so I could throw myself in his arms and plead with him to give us another chance. I don't know that I've ever shared with anyone that I even came that close to making that two-hour drive after the breakup; if I did, they probably would've stolen my keys from me, and rightfully so. I wound find myself so many times glancing out my front door, knowing that he had the code to the gate to drive onto my property and hoping I would see him walk around the corner of my parents' house to come up to my house. I knew my family probably didn't think about the fact that he had the code to our gate, and I almost told them so they could change it. But I didn't. I held onto that one destructive thought, *What if?*

The what-ifs plagued me for what seemed like an eternity. What if he came back? What if he changed and we could repair our relationship? What if I had confronted him sooner? Would we have been able to make it work if I did? What if I will be forever stuck in this terrible place of still being addicted to him? What if I'm never able to stop loving him?

For so many months, I battled sleep deprivation, not being able to fall asleep until some time past 3:00 a.m. and napping here and there throughout the day just to be able to function. The few hours I was able to sleep were anything but restful as one dream of him after another would wake me up, and I would open my eyes most mornings to find that I had once again been crying in my sleep. The intense need to talk to him every night and the dread of being tortured during slumber by the ever-present image of him chased away any inclination to sleep. All waking hours were spent fighting the desire to run back to him, and missing him so much that the pain of it made me nauseous prevented me from being able to eat decently. Through that time, I dropped over ten pounds and had a good bit of hair loss due to the overwhelming stress. My energy was absolutely depleted, and I barely made it through every work day without dropping my head on my desk and falling into an exhausted slumber. I saw reminders of him in everything, and every one of them made me ache to be with him once again; so much so that my head spun. Tears were my constant companion, and all my headaches turned into one continuous migraine. I felt like I was losing my mind.

I'm going to get real here. As terrible as this may sound, it would've been easier for me to hate him. It would've been so wrong, but part of me believes I would've been able to move on, heal, and forgive faster if I did. But no, that addictive love lingered in the depths of my heart for far too long and made the sudden separation between us that much harder.

Because the longing to reach out to him was unbearable, I had to eventually make the hard decision of removing that temptation once and for all. It took some time for me to be able to do this, but I deleted it all. Everything from his phone number, text and Facebook message threads, and little things like his Amazon and Hulu login info to all of our pictures and videos. I threw out the things he gave me and even went so far as to comb through every text thread with family and friends to delete any pictures sent there. Basically, the only thing I couldn't remove was the memory of where he lived and how to get there (honestly, it was only the Holy Spirit that kept me from making the terrible mistake of driving those familiar back roads to his house).

The night I deleted everything was all at once both a healing balm to my shattered heart yet another painful tear to add to the wounds already accumulated. While part of me was relieved to finally get to the point of being able to destroy the reminders, another part was resisting and fighting full force against what I knew I should do. Painstakingly going through every message, every photo and video, I relived for over two hours both the highs and lows of what used to be and battled the desire to hold tightly to the mirage of what I believed was a love to last forever. Removing my last link to the man who had my heart eliminated the temptation to contact him but felt as if I was abruptly extracting the last knife in my heart. Little did I know that the wound, although cleared, would continue to bleed out and throb for some time to come and leave scars so thick, evidence of a heartbreak so clear, that only the grace of God could remove.

Boundaries and Purity Culture

So I'm about to use a word that makes most people cringe these days—purity. Yeah, I'm going there. Purity culture has become toxic over the years in that it has become a strict list of rules to be applied the same way to every person with the looming message of an irreversible fall from grace if you slip. The way purity is typically addressed in our churches creates immense pressure on following stringent rules to avoid premarital sex yet no explanation as to why, a need to determine how close to the edge of the boundary you can get but fear of breaking a rule with the repercussion of harsh judgment, and a severe lack of focus on being pure of heart as well as physically.

If you've been taught that purity is just a laundry list of rules with no grace, please know it's not supposed to be this way. This is not what the heart behind purity should be.

I won't share what my boundaries in relationships are because what I'm comfortable with doing may not be wise for another person or vice versa. Your boundaries should be based on what you are convicted about.

In the very early stages of our relationship, as in thirty minutes before my ex asked me to be his girlfriend, I wanted to be sure we were clear on physical boundaries if we were to keep dating. Needing him to not think I was cool with anything and wanting to see what he was comfortable with if he just so happened to be stricter than me, I asked him what his feelings about it were. I shared that I'm waiting for marriage and what I was and wasn't okay with in a dating relationship.

They say hindsight is twenty-twenty, and you learn your biggest lessons from your mistakes. I'm here to say this is true. The conversation between us that day should have raised a red flag for me, but because I decided to give him the benefit of the doubt, I let it slide. And here was the red flag I missed: I had to be the one to set these boundaries. He did not take the lead in this, and even though the line drawn was respected, I had to draw it myself. This massive warning I missed eventually led to a relationship that showcased passivity from him, the weight of making our relationship work falling on my shoulders, and much later on, a growing feeling that he was unhappy about my decision to save sex for marriage.

I don't say all of that to imply that that he was pushing for more than I was willing to give; he truly did respect my boundaries throughout our relationship and never once made me feel uncomfortable, and I'm so thankful for that. I do say all of that though to encourage the women reading this to not settle for a man who is just going to respect your wishes and play along with a possible hope that you'll cave eventually; instead, date the man who desires just as much as you to stay pure in your relationship and will lead in this.

I'm going to put this bluntly. If both people in a relationship are not convicted in physical boundaries, when the one who is convicted has a weak moment, the other who is not convicted will be unable to be relied upon to make up for the lack. I've been blunt; now let me get blunt *and* personal. Even though my ex-boyfriend and I did not cross a line and we did not do anything that makes me feel guilty and weighed down with regret, we did toe the line at times. It was nothing that makes me look back and think, *That was clearly wrong,* because there is no cut-and-dried list of things one should and shouldn't do in dating as it is dependent on the person and their convictions (extramarital sex being the only clear biblical rule). However, I had *my* personal convictions, and we definitely flirted with that line. I inevitably had days, as we all do because we are human, that I didn't feel near as strong in those convictions as I did when we first began to date. And on those days, I knew I couldn't rely on him to be the counterweight to balance us out. So we pushed the boundaries often and struggled to not do something we'd regret.

I do not say all of that to try to bring light to the fact that we didn't go too far physically or that we did it perfectly in order to receive a pat on my shoulder. We did not do it perfectly, and I have the scars marking my heart to prove it. I say all of that to encourage you to date someone who will be responsible in pursuing purity with you, for you, and for themselves. It won't be perfect and there will be times when neither of you feel like sticking with it, but it is possible. And the end result of purity being brought into marriage, whether that is with them or with someone else, is beautiful.

On a related note, if you or the person you are with have had a past of not being pure in relationships, you *can* pursue purity again. According to 2 Corinthians 5:17, "If anyone is in Christ, he is a new creation. The old has passed away; behold, the new has come." There is redemption and forgiveness found in Christ, not through anything we have done but only because of His mercy and love for us (Titus

3:4–7). Your life can be turned around and you can pursue what God has called you to do with the lent strength of Jesus.

Soul Ties

A new term going around is *soul ties*. Googling this provides many different descriptions (some wilder than others), but the basic definition is an intense connection between two people. Per crosswalk.com, *a soul tie is a deep bond with someone that affects your soul. Our souls are the immaterial parts of us: our emotions, our thoughts, and our desires.*[1]

While there are many different kinds of soul ties, such as connections formed with best friends or family, the strongest of these soul ties are caused by romantic relationships with sexual intimacy being the most bonding. They are easily formed when we give pieces of ourselves away, whether emotionally or physically, and when these are severed, it is immensely painful and difficult to recover from. There is pain that comes with a splintered relationship no matter the type of connection.

And even though *soul tie* is a relatively new term, the concept is biblical.

We can know that these strong connections are biblical because we see in 1 Samuel 18 that David and Jonathan had a tie to each other through their friendship and were closer than blood brothers. When Jonathan was killed, David deeply mourned over the loss (2 Sam. 1). Fast forward to John 11 where we see a second example of a soul tie with the death of Lazarus. Jesus, even though He knew Lazarus would die and knew He would resurrect him when He entered the city of Bethany, still wept and mourned because of His love for His close friend. The loss was still painful to Him, although He was God and knew exactly what would take place.

If the Bible provides us with examples of the pain of these severed intimate relationships, we can take hope that in our own pain caused by the loss of those close to us, we are grieving exactly as

---

[1]   https://www.crosswalk.com/faith/spiritual-life/are-soul-ties-biblical.html

God made us to grieve. It is healthy to mourn the loss of a person you loved, someone you thought would be around for life, a close relationship that held your heart. This is normal. We were created to form these soul ties with people. We were created for community, for close friendships, and for romantic relationships. This is just a part of our beautiful design, and part of that design is to allow yourself to feel the pain of loss and grieve what once was.

Healing Takes Time

If I had to give just one piece of advice for anyone going through a breakup or any kind of heartache, it would be this: Give yourself time and space to grieve, allow yourself to feel all the wild emotions coursing through you, and please don't beat yourself up when the little things bring everything rushing back to the surface.

Nobody really talks much about the small details after a breakup. It's not typical to share about the feeling of going insane from the barrage of pain and emotions. You don't hear much about the little things that are held onto so tightly because if they were to be lost, you'd lose that last precious thread of connection.

Nobody warns you of the way life will be when it's over. Seeing a stranger in the grocery store who smiles like your ex and feeling a pain slice through your chest so sharp you almost double over. Driving by a previous date spot and spending the remainder of your drive home struggling to see past the tears and in a complete emotional fog, wondering how you made it home safely because you no longer remember driving. The refusal to wash the blankets on your couch or that hoodie you wore when he held you because the scent of his cologne still lingers on them. The way you play back old videos to hear his laugh just one more time, yet one time is never enough. The heart-wrenching loneliness that overcomes you when the future you dreamed about together, the days planned out, the life you envisioned, transpire without the other person walking through those days with you and without their hand in yours.

No one speaks of the guilt that washes over you when you have your first truly happy moment because you believed you weren't supposed to be happy without them in your life. The silent sobs and ragged breathing after you realized that you didn't cry any that day which meant you're beginning to move on. The shame that you ever gave your heart away to that person and opened yourself up to be wounded. The burning anger when you finally pitch the gifts given into the trash but immediate regret that same night when you miss them so fiercely and want to cling to some reminder of a love past. There is no talk of the intense need to see their face, once so beloved, one last time after the pictures have been deleted and the maddening scramble to comb through the archives just to find that fulfilling the desire to see them simply led to an even deeper ache in your soul.

The midnight breakdowns, the screams into your pillow at 1:00 a.m., the mind-numbing daze you fall into at 2:00 a.m., the 3:00 a.m. sheer exhaustion as you stare blankly at the ceiling, and 4:00 a.m. tortured dreams of the person you loved only to start the cycle anew at 7:00 a.m. with puffy eyes and a raging migraine.

Nobody prepares you for this, yet it's all so real. The complexity of what is taking place inside your heart is confusing, infuriating, and absolutely excruciating. And please believe what I'm about to share because it took me so very long to understand this and to stop belittling myself.

You're not crazy or dramatic for feeling this way.

You're not crazy for having a normal response to the sudden hole shot through your heart. When you love someone so deeply and completely, it would be abnormal to not feel that way. Experiencing this does not make you weak; it makes you human. It eventually makes you stronger, even though it's impossible to see in the moment.

The trap is not the emotions we face but what we do with them. Are we allowing ourselves to sit in our grief longer than we should? While there is no given time frame of moving into a place of healing, there does come a point when we have to push through the pain to get to the other side and not allow the grief to hold us back any longer. There will come a day when we must confront head-on what harmed us and fight back the lies and pain with the Truth of God.

Web of Lies

In the darkest moments, one question after another would bombard her and threaten to pull her even further into the black abyss of depression and mind games that the enemy was playing with her.

"Why wasn't I good enough for him?"

"What about me made him want to leave?"

"Why couldn't I make him stay and fight for me?"

"When did he stop loving me?"

"Did he ever love me?"

"Will I ever be truly loved?"

The still of every night brought unwanted visitors who took up residence in the home of her soul. Fear introduced itself as the one whose message is that of permanent isolation and dreams that will remain just that. Dreams. Loneliness would come traipsing in, seemingly from all entrances, and settle in for an extended stay. It would turn the lights off and bring with it an uncomfortable silence. Pounding at the door was anger, demanding justice and a sound reason why life hadn't changed in the way it was thought to change. And then there was doubt. Doubt crept in through the window and didn't make its presence known until she tripped over it as if it were a rope pulled taut to make her stumble and stay put in a crumbled heap on the cold, hard floor.

As she fell victim to this downward spiral and cruel attacks, the days would seem so bleak, the wound so profound she feared it would never close up. Time passed in a haze. Each morning started with a dread of facing another day, and each night brought a renewed sense of loss and loneliness. Pasting on a fake smile, she would proceed to live with the pretense that she was okay, that she was moving on and happy. Beneath that thin, almost-crumbling veneer, however, she struggled with the lies continuing to beat her down. She fought to find a moment of peace, but every desperate attempt failed.

Life seemed to move on, but she found herself with one foot in the past. Part of her heart was still unrecovered. The past was quicksand and threatened to take more of her than what it already had. She marveled at how she was able to get even that much of herself out of the morass but simultaneously disheartened that it continued to ensnare a portion of her. Feeling as though this piece of her was encased in concrete, immovable and irreparable, she strained to free herself from the trap. Thoughts and emotions pelted her mind and heart, and dodging these bullets while maintaining a peaceful outward facade left her struggling for her next breath. Utterly exhausted. Trapped in a constant emotional hell. Falling deeper into the ominous pit of depression. Scared of the continued darkness in the home of her soul.

Round and round again, the lies would send her mind into a tailspin and plague her. She was stuck on the front lines of a war she felt she was losing. As if trying to go upstream in a mob, she got nowhere. Frozen in place while strength was being robbed from her as the lies struck her repeatedly and the undesirable visitors in her soul continued to make their presence known.

Fake Smiles and Hidden Tears

I've dealt with anxiety for years. It wasn't really anything that concerned me as it was never crippling, but like most people, it was there. Depression, on the other hand, was not something I had experienced or at least noticed myself going through. Yes, life would deal me some hard moments, but long bouts of despondency never entered the equation. Not until I was left floundering after the breakup.

The initial few days after we broke up, I would confide some of my feelings and pain to the people closest to me. While that time just emphasized what amazing family and friends I have and how supportive and loving they are, I began to feel guilty talking about my problems. Through no fault of their own and entirely the fault of the lies I began to believe, I started to close myself off by the end of that first week. I took on the "suck it up" mentality, replaced the tears with what I hoped to be a serene smile, and prayed my high-coverage concealer would mask the dark circles under my eyes. I acted as if I was moving on and at peace with the situation, but in reality, I was stuck in a constant state of depression and falling prey to the lies that steadily plagued me. My heart was shattered, the shards of what remained were frozen, and the darkness that was creeping into my soul from all sides was beginning to overtake me. And I felt like a fraud, pretending to be okay when, in reality, I was the furthest thing from it.

I've felt like I've had to fake it when I'm around others. Everyone is checking up on me, and I appreciate it more than words can say. But I've just wanted to be completely alone. The days go by so slowly because we're not talking anymore. I dread nights…Little things remind me of him and I feel the pain all over…Everyone keeps saying he's not worth crying over and I deserve so much better…but I don't think they realize how much I loved him. I hate the way this has wrecked me and hate the fact that I know I'll be tempted to take him back if he ever asks.

Above was a snippet from my journal during the beginning of the darkest season I have ever gone through. I had never experienced loneliness like that before, and the depression that set in was new for me. I pushed everyone around me away as much as I could, and only very few people saw that I was struggling. Even those who knew didn't know exactly how bad it was and about the nights I would sit on my bathroom floor and sob or the struggle to see my computer screen during work through the constant tears. Nobody knew about the terrifying numbness that was quickly overtaking me. Every morning was an internal fight to get out of bed as I found myself with nothing to look forward to when I would wake up. Because I couldn't find the motivation to continue life as normal, there were countless times I was tempted to call my boss to quit my job on the spot or almost skip out on family events. Making excuses when I did go out with my family or close friends, I would cut my time with them as short as possible so I could escape to the lonely quiet of my house. I would spend the long, reclusive hours of the night lying in my bed, sleepless and staring at the ceiling while my brain spun a web of lies so intricate that it would take months to untangle. I was being tugged into a pit so dark and so lonely with nothing to accompany me but the lies I was becoming enslaved to and the doubts that threatened to tear me away from the one source of freedom and truth that would never fail me.

It's All a Bunch of Lies

Lie: I will never be truly loved.
Truth: "God shows His love for us in that while we were still sinners, Christ died for us" (Rom. 5:8 ESV).

Like most people, over the years, life has dealt some hard moments. Whether that was losing some friends due to moving in different areas in life, typical work and school stress, or difficult health issues in my family, they stung and were hard. Even through those times, I knew I've always been unbelievably blessed in being surrounded by the most loving family and friends. Ultimately, I had Jesus's love to constantly lean on. I knew who I was and to whom I belonged.

But somewhere along the way I lost sight of that.

More than likely, I started believing this lie before I met my ex. Yes, I had blamed him for a time, but in reality, his feigned love only peeled back the layers of my heart and soul and exposed what had previously taken root in me. I was seeking my identity in temporary, humanly love over the eternal, flawless love found only in Jesus. I was looking for stability in my relationships with family and friends and came up lacking every time. I didn't realize this until the love and security from one of the most important people in my life was ripped away.

I knew the way he left had severely destroyed my trust, but I didn't think that distrust and hurt would bleed into my other relationships with the people I've always loved and trusted. It was months before I could see that the lie of never truly being loved was taking root and shaping my life. Not until one incident that caused some minor hurt left me questioning the relationships with people who knew and loved me. Just a small misunderstanding and lack of communication from someone close to me who I felt like I hadn't seen enough of through those long months brought to the surface the fear of not being loved. I questioned every motive behind every action and word from every person in my life. I wondered if those around me only stayed because they felt they had to, and I struggled with feeling as if every relationship I had was going to suddenly crash and burn as well.

Honestly, after that very minuscule hurt from that one miscommunication, I felt like a brat who didn't get her way and thought everyone was against me. I felt myself rapidly put up walls in order to close everyone off from me. To prevent getting hurt and due to the fear of finding more relationships built on pretense and obligation, I began to distance myself. I refused to let the people closest to me get a glimpse of what was really going on in my head and to see the warped thinking that had suddenly revealed itself. I soon began to find myself becoming increasingly bitter to love and trust. I felt so guilty for the new pathways my brain was beginning to form with this lie, so I knew this mindset had to be reframed quickly before it really did destroy the relationships I valued.

The only way I found to combat this lie was to fully immerse myself in the love of Jesus. If we want to live free of the fear of unrequited, fabricated love and instead believe that we can have people in our lives that love us for who we are, we have to look to the source of true love. We have to accept that in this life, we will not find perfect love from people. Yes, there are definitely those who love beautifully and selflessly, but ultimately, this too will have disappointments and hurts that come with it because we are all human. We can avoid the discouragement that comes along with this by looking to the flawless love freely given by God. If we root ourselves so deeply in the love of God and find identity and security in Him, we will be able to love those around us without regard to whether or not they will love us in return.

First John 4:7–21 highlights the overwhelming love of God, the manifestation of that love, how we are able to then love others from His outflow of love, and the lack of fear in perfected love. Lots of love, huh? But that's just the reality of it when we open ourselves up to the truth of God's absolutely flawless love for us and allow it to then carry out into our relationships on earth.

If we confess that Jesus is the Son of God and believe in His saving grace (v.15), we are then born of God (v.7) and are given the Holy Spirit. We then know that we abide in God and that He is in us and with us (v.13). Out of abiding (remaining/dwelling) in Jesus's love, we are able to extend love to others because of the Holy Spirit living in us. Because nobody has seen God face-to-face, His love is seen and carried through His people, thus being perfected in us. Not because of what we have done or how we love, but because of how He loves us. And we can be confident that fear does not exist where His love is.

So what does this mean for us and how do we live in light of this? It means that in this life, we recognize that we are in a broken world with broken people but rest in the fact that God's people, although not perfect themselves, showcase His perfect love. We remain constantly in His love by spending our time with Him, living in obedience to Him out of gratitude and love for Him, and loving the people He places in our life and letting others love us, making allowance for grace when they inevitably mess up just as we will. This also means living without the fear of failed love because we are ultimately secure in Jesus's love for us and that eternity is waiting where we will be whole and complete when we finally see Him face-to-face.

Lie: I am not really beautiful.
Truth: "I am fearfully and wonderfully made" (Ps. 139:14 ESV).

Two nights before the breakup, I confessed to my mom that I thought one of our many problems was that he wasn't thrilled with the way I look. And here is my twisted reasoning for this lie. Although he would compliment me and make me feel beautiful, he would only see me done up with, at the very least, some foundation and eyeliner. The last time he had ever seen me (as in the day before our relationship took a turn for the worse) was the warmest day we had since we had been together, and because it felt like summer was coming, we decided to go swimming. His last perception of me had been in a swimsuit with not a hint of makeup on. And, well, because of my bad shoulder, I hadn't been to the gym in a while, so I definitely wasn't "summer body" ready. I admit, I was self-conscious.

I shared with him that I was feeling slightly insecure because it was the first time he was seeing me that way. His response while not meeting my eye? "You look fine." Not exactly the most convincing or encouraging statement I had ever heard. So you can imagine the conclusions I jumped to when I was struggling to figure out where we went wrong and how I went back through conversations and discovered that after that day, I never heard the words, "You're beautiful," from him ever again. I was convinced he was no longer attracted to me and found someone better looking. I didn't and still to this day don't know if that was a reason or not. It could've been, but regardless, I started to believe a lie that my physical appearance was all that mattered.

As time went on, my insecurities in regards to my appearance intensified. My thought was, *I can't let him be the hot ex.* Petty, right? Three weeks after the breakup, I tried to change my eating habits and got on an exercise kick. Both are great to implement as long as they're backed by the correct motive and done well. My new eating habits basically meant I was eating less (I had just gotten to the point of being able to stomach food again, so this wasn't a smart move), and the exercise would've been a healthy habit if I were eating normally. At baseline, I'm on the lower end of normal weight, so the ten-plus pounds I lost put me decidedly underweight. I got an appointment as soon as I could with my hair stylist and changed up my hair. I switched my personal Instagram from private to public because if he happened to make an account and search for me, I wanted him to see what he was missing and that I was doing great. But I wasn't doing great. I was really a walking skeleton with a killer hairstyle who was slowly dying inside.

My focus shifted solely to my physical appearance instead of what was internal. I looked to change things about the shape of my body instead of the shape of my heart. Pinpointing all my physical flaws, I was blind to the flaws in my character. I thought if I looked a certain way, more beautiful or more fit, then maybe he would regret our relationship going south.

It all caught up to me when I got sick with what I think was the flu, bronchitis, and pink eye combined and took a few weeks to recover, only to get another cold right after. I don't think I've ever been that sick before. Although it sucked, it forced me to stay away from the gym and to eat whatever I could handle, but more importantly, it allowed me to refocus on what needed to change internally. It drove me to see the toxic habits and thought patterns that were molding my life.

I had to reevaluate where I was finding my self-worth. I had to come to grips with the fact that no matter how beautiful someone can make me feel in a given moment, that feeling is only as temporary as the physical appearance that always changes with time. There has to be a solid foundation of confidence in who God made me to be and total trust that He makes no mistakes. Instead of looking in the mirror and picking out what I thought were flaws, I had to look at them and instead thank God for making me that way, even if it might not be my idea of what is beautiful. Who am I to question the work of the Creator? If He says He creates each person amazingly and miraculously (ESV version), then isn't it an insult to Him if we degrade our bodies with our criticizing remarks and disgusted glances in the mirror? I can't imagine how it must break God's heart for Him to look at His beautiful creation drowning in self-hate and depleted God-confidence in who they are, struggling to swim to the surface by using the fatal techniques of comparison and stringent, unhealthy lifestyle changes.

I think we can all admit we struggle with this lie in some form or another. Even those who seem to be enthralled with their own appearances still battle insecurity on some level. We live in a world full of comparison. The standard of beauty is ever-changing as media tells us what is currently trending, who has been voted sexiest man or woman alive, or what we should do to live that perfect, Instagram-worthy life. We live in an airbrushed and photoshopped world that bombards our already overwhelmed hearts with unrealistic ideals and unattainable lifestyles. Society tells us to strive to become the epitome of fashion and wealth but leave our souls to rot. Instead of embracing our physical appearances and developing our character, we embrace our character and attempt to develop our physical appearances. It's soul-sucking and absolutely toxic.

Moving the focus from looking like those girls on our Instagram feeds or the ripped guys at the gym to looking more like Jesus is a daily choice. It's a continual mindset shift from self-depreciation to gratefulness for the beautiful way you were created. Learning to be confident in who you were created to be is a process full of patience, grace with yourself, and trust that God makes no mistakes. You and I were created in His image (Gen. 1:27) and for a purpose (Eph. 2:10), and we can draw assurance from that and live in light of this truth.

Lie: I will never heal and be able to love again.
Truth: "He heals the brokenhearted and binds up their wounds" (Ps. 147:3 ESV).

In the most intense moments of pain with lingering aftereffects as time went on, the growing belief that my heart was permanently damaged and the thread of doubt that falling in love once more was no longer imaginable wove themselves so deeply into my life. Every instance of someone sharing with me that they think I'd be a good fit for a guy they knew or whenever I was asked about my love life, I'd immediately fall into the lie that there was no possible way I could love someone the way I had once loved my ex-boyfriend. I would be instantly discouraged when a bad day of missing him left me shaking with ill-suppressed emotion and relentless tears. Knowing it wouldn't be fair to enter another relationship when I was still so hung up on my ex, I refused to entertain the possibility of loving once again, even in the very distant future. The phrase, "Time heals all wounds," was a sentiment that incessantly mocked me. It was as if the cliché expression was really saying, *Time heals all wounds... Well, except maybe yours.*

Although there was no jealousy toward other couples in happy, healthy relationships, there was an ever-present ache from the reminder that the person I had loved walked out of my life. I could be genuinely happy for those around me but still have a looming sadness over the thought that I would never be able to be in that position of loving someone so fully and deeply as I once had. I began to believe that the man that swept into my life and stole my heart but in an instant left just as quickly as he arrived would always have a piece of me that would remain unrecoverable. Healing seemed far-fetched and opening myself up to love again completely unrealistic. It was as if I was stuck in a rut of constantly thinking about and missing him with fears of remaining in that place pulling me in deeper.

But even though the process of healing seemed bleak and hopeless at times, it wouldn't stay this way. I wouldn't stay this way.

There's a popular analogy of God's plan for His children and the way we view it, but I never understood it more than I have recently. Our lives are like a tapestry. On one side, the side we see and experience, is a jumbled mess of intersecting, tangled threads. They do not appear to have any purpose, and the image we see is anything but beautiful. It's confusing and a pain to look at when attempting to trace the paths of those threads. But then you flip the tapestry. On that other side, the one we can't fully see, is a magnificent piece of art. All the bunches of thread actually do possess a purpose and reflect the intricate handiwork of the Creator. The complicated situations and the days filled with raw pain and seemingly unending difficulties combine with the truly beautiful, joy-filled times to display an amazing story of God's sovereignty and unique plan for each of our lives.

The pain is oh-so-real and at times agonizing, but it is temporary. As Christians, we aren't promised easy, carefree lives (John 16:33), but we are promised the peace of God that surpasses all understanding (Phil. 4:7) and a coming day when there will be no more pain or sorrow (Rev. 21:4).

I can say all of this but still question how knowing eternity will be pain-free makes the present any more bearable and how this can translate into practical life. It doesn't change the heartache, but it does give hope. Healing does happen with time, yes, but ultimately it is only possible through the work of God. We take it one day at a time, and through each day, through each minute, we recognize our need for Jesus and our inability to live this life without Him. We learn to trust that He is writing a beautiful story for our lives, one that is infinitely better than we can ever imagine, and take comfort in His love that's readily available to each of us. We run into His arms and allow Him to lovingly care for the broken pieces of our hearts that we are unable to put back together. We begin to believe that, through Jesus, redemption is available, and what we once thought would be impossible, can one day become a beautiful reality.

Lie: There are no more decent, godly men, and I will always be their last choice.
Truth: "Husbands, love your wives, as Christ loved the church and gave Himself up for her" (Eph. 5:25 ESV).

Every time someone would tell me the right man would come along one day, I'd smile and outwardly agree, but secretly I would scoff at the cliché expression and mentally ask if they had any clue as to what the dating pool is like these days. The few decent guys were quickly being snatched up. And the ones that were left? Well, let's just say they made me more than happy to stay single.

You'd think that as time went on and I found myself moving further from my past relationship, I would start to believe again that decent men existed. Nope. Two men entered my life a few months after my breakup, one right after another, who both further pushed me away from any hope of meeting a good guy. While one was playing the manipulation game and the other was going between ghosting and trying to hit me up in the middle of the night, my expectations lowered drastically. And those expectations were already six feet under to begin with. The drama with these two men brought to the surface a deep wound that came from my previous relationship, one that I never dealt with.

Not too long before we broke up, my ex decided to tell me some of the details of his dating app experience which included how he swiped right on literally every girl, without even glancing at the profiles, just to get a match. Okay, *ouch*. So ours wasn't a story of him seeing my profile and swiping right based off of what he saw and read, but all right, moving on. The real cut was when he told me that he only went out on that first date with me because I was the only girl to accept and basically shared that I was the convenient option in his desperation for a girlfriend. He was getting tired of being single and went with the only girl who would give him a chance. And I ended up being that girl because the others in his roster didn't go out with him. When he shared that heart-wrenching piece of information with me about how we came to be together, I was determined to forgive and forget. Although that barb cut deeply in my heart, my mind told me that it didn't matter because we loved each other, that it would all work out now that we were together, and I refused to believe the reality that he would leave once a better option came along. So I put on my rose-colored glasses once again and continued on with our relationship and with my life, not knowing that the wound inflicted spanned several layers of my heart and would suddenly reveal itself in a way that would cripple me and at a time when I thought I was in a healthy state. I didn't realize just how badly the lie that there was something wrong with me and that I would always be the last choice or convenient option had infiltrated and taken root in my soul.

Fast forward to almost seven months later when I felt as if I was finally in a healthy place, but it all came rushing back in with a fierce tenacity and resulted in an explosion of unruly emotions and once-forgotten hurts. The damage from that night seven months prior that I never faced and believed that I had forgotten was really lurking under the surface of my life, covertly feeding my thoughts and spreading throughout my heart, only growing from additional experiences. You see, an ignored blow of your ex telling you that you were only his girlfriend because you were the convenient choice and he was desperate, and then you add in a guy who slides into your DMs, ghosts you, and only hits you up in the middle of the night when he's exhausted all his other options (and let's not forget other men before and after this who also treated you as a last resort with the games they played), makes for one heck of a toxic mindset. It was a mindset that I allowed to form and didn't properly deal with until everything in me exploded.

After a particularly rough week of dealing with the emotional baggage from my ex and trying to figure out how to introduce some distance with a guy to whom I was just another girl on his roster, while also handling an unexpected 1:00 a.m. message from another man I thought was out of my life, I was done. I told both of my best friends, "I'm absolutely fed up with men. I can't do this anymore." It seemed that the only guys I attracted were jerks, and I couldn't get the thought out of my head that I was always last choice for the guys that supposedly wanted to pursue me.

Logically, I knew there were good guys somewhere. After all, I had friends getting married to some of them, so I knew they existed. But my heart wouldn't accept it. Every hurt and every disappointment from one failed relationship and one failed potential after another just seemed to compound until my heart became callous and bitter. The idea of a godly relationship became laughable and futile, and the concept that I was so much better off alone became believable and safe. I began to utterly despise the thought of dating again.

My best friends both saw the concerning bitterness that was building in me. One was praying for my heart to soften and encouraging me to expand my community to see that there are good men out there. My other best friend and my mom both dropped a bombshell of truth that opened my eyes and pulled me from the toxic mindset I had adopted. My best friend sent me a text saying, "One day, you're going to find a guy and you won't be their first choice, you'll be their only choice…A biblical marriage represents Christ and the church…He didn't think of the church as a second choice. So if God's gonna bless you with marriage one day, then He's going to send you a godly guy who will see you first before all the other girls. Even when he does see the other girls, you'll still be the only one he wants." The next day, my mom unknowingly reiterated this when she saw how deeply this all had damaged me. And since then, my perspective has shifted and the lie, although still sneaking in at times, no longer has its roots embedded in me.

While it's true that there are numerous people whose only goal is to gain something from a relationship, thriving on the games they play and the disrespect they have for others, there can still be hope for a godly spouse one day (I know this is not one-sided and that the good guys have to deal with women acting this way as well). Even though some days it's hard to believe, I can still hold onto the hope of God placing a man in my life who is genuine, godly, and will love me for who I am because he will look to Jesus for that ability. Our standards can and should remain high because the right person will meet them, not perfectly by any means, but will consistently work to meet them and daily choose commitment and love.

Lie: What happened was all my fault.
Truth: "There is therefore now no condemnation for those who are in Christ Jesus" (Rom. 8:1 ESV).

There was a very short period of time when I was angry with my ex and the way he treated me. Sure, the anger was justified, but in those moments, I put all of the blame on him and acted as if I had no fault in our relationship and breakup. However, that anger toward him didn't last long. Because I had believed the best in him for so long and had loved him so deeply, the anger that would creep back in after a remembrance of what happened or an additional piece of the puzzle would fall into place would quickly fade away. It was hard to stay mad at him. Extremely hurt? Yes. Bitter and hateful toward him? Nope.

So the blame shifted solely to me.

I would constantly ask myself what I did wrong, what about me was so bad that he couldn't love me, and why I couldn't see who he truly was from the beginning. I was angry at myself for falling in love with him in the first place and angry at how I apparently couldn't get a guy to stick around. I grew to hate myself for allowing it all to happen, for not being discerning enough to see the warning signs, and for not being able to stand up for myself. And I absolutely despised the way I was not strong enough to move on from him and how I let it all affect me in the way it did and for as long as it did.

Here's the thing. I did make plenty of mistakes in our relationship; there's no escaping that. I don't know how our breakup affected him, but I do know how it affected me. And we were both at fault. At some point though, I knew I had to learn from the past and move on. There had to come a point where I let go of the guilt for my mistakes and the hate toward myself because it became too large a weight to carry around.

Have you ever traveled by yourself by plane? If you have, you know that it's so cumbersome to bring your carry-on luggage with you everywhere you go in the airport. To the restaurants. To the bathroom. You have to put it in the overhead bin yourself. Even lugging it to the rental car place and juggling all your possessions while trying to sign the rental car agreement. By the end of the trip, you're irritated with carrying around the bags and exhausted. The same is true for emotional baggage of guilt and shame.

Carrying around baggage from the past complicates the present and future because your hands are full and you are unable take on anything else. You become too busy trying to balance the pressure from shouldering past remorse that any new relationship that tries to come along is only pushed away and current relationships suffer from neglect. The guilt that keeps you up at night and the paranoia that others are judging you for your choices eat at your soul and you feel unable to escape the darkness that comes along with it. You start to feel like you're going insane from questioning every little decision you make for fear it will end up like a prior situation. It's impossible to continue on with life with this weight on your chest that keeps you from moving forward.

Unlike the physical baggage of suitcases that you are entirely responsible for dealing with, we can hand off the emotional baggage to Someone else. We can check in those bags, but unlike what we do with an airline, we don't have to take them back home with us. There is a way to be free of that weight.

When we lay our burdens down at the feet of Jesus, He is willing and able to take them from us. When we are saved by His grace, we are free from condemnation. He has taken our guilt away. This doesn't mean we don't deal with any consequences of our sin, but the most severe consequence, being separated from God, is taken away. With this freedom from condemnation, we can learn from our mistakes and move forward in life without hesitation and fear.

We are human. We mess up. We sin and regret it. We become blinded to things that will harm us, and we fall into temptation.

Until Jesus's return, we are stuck in these mortal bodies and will constantly fight this war of wanting to do good but sometimes doing what is not good. But we know that, because of Jesus, the war against sin and death is already won. This doesn't give us an excuse to sin, but instead it empowers us to use the freely given power from the Holy Spirit to keep trying our best to follow Jesus. It sets us free from the dark bondage of guilt and shame that keeps us reliving our past mistakes day in and day out. It opens the door to the shining, glorious light of Jesus's love and His work on the cross to pay the penalty of our sins once and for all. Instead of becoming bogged down in the dirty mire of our mistakes, we can dance joyfully and freely in the beauty of forgiveness and grace.

Lie: God doesn't care what happens to me.
Truth: "How precious to me are your thoughts, O God! How vast is the sum of them! If I would count them, they are more than the sand. I awake, and I am still with you" (Ps. 139:17–18 ESV).

Probably the worst lie out of all that I fell prey to was this one. In my anger and deep hurt, I blamed God for taking away the man I loved, allowing me to end up with a shattered heart and having a completely different plan than what I had in mind. Even though I didn't say or think it outright, I began to believe that He didn't care. Little threads of doubt started to intertwine with what I knew to be true. In my mind, I knew He did care and that He has a much better plan than anything I could ever come up with, but my heart and soul refused to grasp onto that truth.

Very early on into my relationship with my ex, I prayed that dangerous prayer. You know, the one we say but really don't mean? *Lord, if this man is not right for me, then I pray that this doesn't work.* But then later on, I prayed that desperate, completely opposite, prayer repeatedly over two separate time periods. *God, please don't take him from me.* And when He did, I felt like I was given the wrong end of a deal. Didn't He want me to be happy and in a loving relationship that hopefully reflected Jesus? Didn't He see me struggling to continue on with life? How about all those nights I spent sobbing, enduring a new split in my heart with each agonized breath and a new ugly scar that formed with every wound inflicted? I thought He wanted what was best for His children, so why didn't it seem like He cared?

Maybe it was out of God's desire to see me in a happy, healthy relationship He took away the one that actually never reflected His love. Possibly, He knew that the nights I spent with bloodshot eyes and raging migraines would be nothing compared to the lifetime of heartache I would have if I had married my ex. It could be that He felt every bit of that pain I experienced and it saddened Him to see but still had to let me walk through it anyway because He knew it was what would strengthen my faith and cause me to lean on Him. In the Father's care for me and His desire to give me life, He took away the relationship that was slowly killing me. He saw that I was losing myself and that my identity was rapidly deteriorating, so He saved me and allowed me to find myself once more and reestablish my identity firmly in Jesus.

Remember the analogy of the tapestry looking crappy from one side and gorgeous from the other? It's a picture of His sovereignty and power, yes, but also of His infinitely tender care and love for us. Oftentimes, we can't see beyond the moment we are in and unable to know what dangers any given situation may bring. We can't realize the needed growth and character change until we are on the other side of heartache. There is purpose in the pain and through it all, the Father's loving care is indescribable and constantly present, even when we can't see it.

Through the long months, Psalm 139 became my lifeline. Nothing else I can ever write will come remotely close to this remarkable description of God's unfathomable love.

> O Lord, you have searched me and known me! You know when I sit down and when I rise up; you discern my thoughts from afar. You search out my path and my lying down and are acquainted with all my ways. Even before a word is on my tongue, behold, O Lord, you know it

altogether. You hem me in, behind and before, and lay your hand upon me. Such knowledge is too wonderful for me; it is high; I cannot attain it. Where shall I go from your Spirit? Or where shall I flee from your presence? If I ascend to heaven, you are there! If I make my bed in Sheol, you are there! If I take the wings of the morning and dwell in the uttermost parts of the sea, even there your hand shall lead me, and your right hand shall hold me. If I say, "Surely the darkness shall cover me, and the light about me be night," even the darkness is not dark to you; the night is bright as the day, for darkness is as light with you. For you formed my inward parts; you knitted me together in my mother's womb. I praise you, for I am fearfully and wonderfully made. Wonderful are your works; my soul knows it very well. My frame was not hidden from you, when I was being made in secret, intricately woven in the depths of the earth. Your eyes saw my unformed substance; in your book were written, every one of them, the days that were formed for me, when as yet there was none of them. How precious to me are your thoughts, O God! How vast is the sum of them! If I would count them, they are more than the sand. I awake, and I am still with you. Oh that you would slay the wicked, O God! O men of blood, depart from me! They speak against you with malicious intent; your enemies take your name in vain. Do I not hate those who hate you, O Lord? And do I not loathe those who rise up against you? I hate them with complete hatred; I count them my enemies. Search me, O God, and know my heart! Try me and know my thoughts! And see if there be any grievous way in me, and lead me in the way everlasting!

Root Issues

As I read yet another rejection email for a job position, this one being a job I was really holding out hope for, my eyes started to water (y'all are really going to think I'm a crybaby by this point, but I promise I'm not!). Why on earth was I tearing up about an email that said, "I'm sorry, but unfortunately, you're not the right fit for this position." I've gone through this so many times over my adult years and know good and well how applying for jobs go; I should be used to it by now because it's nothing personal. But there I was, sitting at my desk with tears running down my face. I knew I had to make a choice. I could either sit there and wallow in my emotions or I could get to the root of why one minor disappointment affected me as it did.

Everything that has gone on this year has taught me many things. One of them being to not suppress my emotions but to allow myself to feel them and ultimately find the root and deal with the core issue. The more I stop myself from stuffing everything down emotionally, the easier it is to trace those emotions to the cause.

If you're anything like me in regards to not wanting to face what you're really feeling or even attempt to name what you're feeling, I've lost you with that last paragraph. Let me try this again.

The old me would've gotten that rejection email, felt the tears build up, and immediately start thinking of something positive to distract myself. I would've probably gotten angry with myself for being a baby about something so minuscule and continue through my day berating myself. The problem with this is that while distraction may work for a time and the internal scolding may keep the tears at bay, all this is doing is just causing disappointments and anger to build up and smolder inside. It's like banking a fire with a layer of ash, but one gust of wind can bring it roaring back to life. There is a deeper issue that should be addressed but has instead been covered up. What this has looked like for me is appearing subdued and moody to others, unsatisfaction with life in general, and frankly, depression. Sound familiar?

More often, we tend to put blame on external factors for our unruly emotions instead of finding the true source. Don't get me wrong; physiological factors contribute to this, but sometimes, they are not the main issue. I'll be the first to admit that PMS has had me down in the dumps more times than I can count. So, yes, there are definitely times when it's not a spiritual issue; it's physiological. Sometimes, depression is genetic and isn't something we can control with finding root issues in our beliefs but something that may need to be managed medically. But in this case with me, it was not physiological.

Here is the trail I had to follow when it came to the rejection email. *What triggered the tears?* Another job that I was excited about fell through. *What emotions was I feeling?* Disappointment and discouragement, anger and frustration. Normal emotions but their depth and the tears involved were not typical. *Was there something more that was causing these negative emotions, something underlying that has been going on?* I was missing having my ex a phone call away to share my work frustrations with and lean on for moral support and angry once again that my plans fell through (now we're getting somewhere). *The root issue?* Loneliness and discontent.

I know that not every negative emotion is that deep and can be traced back to a major root issue, but we have to do the hard work of delving in and sorting through the emotions to get to the source. And once we get to that source, which is most likely a lie that we are believing, we have to combat it with the truth from God's Word. The process is not easy nor is the result immediate. Sometimes it can look like months of struggle, but I can promise you that the end result of a lie from the enemy being replaced with a truth from God is so worth the time and effort.

Don't Look to the Left

Memories can come back in an unbidden rush. Stepping into a place, feeling the atmosphere, and seeing familiar sights can bring a strong sense of déjà vu. Before she knows it, she relives something she had been striving to forget.

Something so simple as a booth in a crowded restaurant can cause the little details to come flooding into her mind. The comfort of holding his arm. The flirty expressions across the dinner table. Uncontrollable laughter at a corny joke. The soft brush of his lips against hers while his hand is running through her hair. Conversations that allow more glimpses into each other's souls and entangles her heart more than she thought possible.

Similar to pulling a thread, it continues to unravel. One recollection leads to another and yet another until all of it plays repeatedly like a tape. The replay is tantalizing and tempts her to dwell on every memory, but ultimately, she's left in a state of melancholy. She fights against it. She struggles to suppress the memories and push them to the back of her mind, but they keep breaking through her defenses. They mock her by saying that this is all she has left of her failed love. They stream in faster and faster until she's stuck in the midst of a swirling vortex of unwanted flashbacks, battling for her next breath as she resists the torrent of tears fighting for release.

No one knows the dizzying effects she's experiencing because of this memory trap. Composure is difficult to maintain, but she uses every ounce of her dwindling strength to prevent others from seeing her emotional nosedive. Praying constantly for self-control, she counts down the minutes until she's alone and can let the tears flow.

Even though the setback is frustrating, she allows herself to cry and acknowledge the emotions, and finally, the playback of memories seems to ease. As she looks at her reflection of red eyes and blotchy face in the mirror, she admonishes herself yet again about falling into nostalgia and prays that the next time a memory resurfaces, it won't strike as hard.

Erase the Tape

It's going to be okay.

It's not a big deal.

You're being a baby about this. You've been to this restaurant a hundred times before. This is no different.

I gave myself this pep talk from the time I woke up one morning in early August until my family was seated at the restaurant that evening. Did it work? Sure, until halfway through dinner when those words lost all credibility. I wasn't okay, it was a big deal to me, and despite trying my hardest to think of all of the other many times I had gone there over the years, all I could think about was the one time I had gone in the previous spring. That night might as well have been played on the TV screen at the bar across from where I was sitting; that's how vivid my mind was replaying those memories.

And I couldn't find the freaking remote to stop the tape.

I was already dealing with some negative emotions because I had imagined that week to be much different than what it had turned out to be, but when I found out that my family was having dinner at this particular restaurant, I was determined to not let it bother me. After all, it was just a restaurant I had been to so many times over the years. I had plenty of memories there I could think back to instead of the one I needed to avoid. So, while still mentally repeating my little pep talk, I walked in with my brother and waited for a table and the rest of our family to show up. So far so good.

Don't look to the left…

I kept my eyes either glued to my phone or turned to talk to my brother, who was on my right thankfully. My family arrived, and we got seated to the right side of the restaurant. Great. Not feeling emotional or nostalgic. Still going strong.

Do not look to the left.

We ordered our food, talked, laughed, and had a great time. All the while, I was doing pretty well. I had thought back a couple times to the memory-to-be-avoided, but I was successfully able to move on to other things and not dwell on it.

Until I looked to the left.

You're probably thinking, *What on earth was "to the left" of her?* Just a booth. Nothing special yet I knew that looking that way and seeing where my ex-boyfriend and I had sat one night would trigger a flood of memories—memories of an evening where we felt the most carefree, blissfully in love and not giving thought to who saw, not wanting to leave each other but feeling as if we had our whole lives together in front of us and all the time in the world. It was the simplest of dates, yet it still embodied all my dreams for us and fanned the hope I had for our future.

I looked to the left and saw the couple who walked into the restaurant and sat at that booth much later than intended because she jumped into his arms the moment she saw him, and they would have rather stayed that way instead of going into town. The way that girl hung onto every word he said, clinging to the love she thought she saw in his eyes. How they were lost to the world around them, so much so that the waiter eventually stopped coming around to check on them so they could enjoy their time together. I glimpsed again the late-night talk at her house about anything and everything, the cuddles while they watched a movie or listened to their favorite music, and the prolonged goodbye just to get every second together. The memories of sweet kisses flashed through my mind, and the sound of their laughter as he picked her up and spun her around her kitchen still rang in my ears. That couple was just a memory to serve as bittersweet torture, and I couldn't get away from them.

After months of wondering why that one night stood out to me so much, I've finally realized the reason. That night was the one time we were together when we weren't overshadowed by anything else. On other dates, we had the awkwardness of meeting for the first time and getting to know each other, the stress of balancing a relationship and his difficult career, and deciding what and where to compromise to make "us" work. Other times, we had the dark cloud of disappointments, broken trust, and hidden pasts hovering over us, threatening to drop its deluge any minute. But that evening, we were free from all of that, if just for a few hours. And the bittersweet memories from that night played in my mind on repeat.

I struggled to hang on to my unraveling emotions and refused to fall apart before I made it to the safety and privacy of my house. I'm sure my family was confused about the sudden silence from me, but I knew if I talked too much, I'd break down. And at that point in my life, I was still too full of pride to allow that wall to crumble and let others in on what was going on inside of me.

After some time, I believed I was finally making progress in forgetting him and what we once had together, but two months later proved me wrong. I soon came to understand that stuffing the feelings down and refusing to talk through what was tearing me apart was only hindering the healing. Progress wasn't actually happening, and I wasn't forgetting him…

*****

She couldn't ignore the emotional wreck she had become randomly one day when just a song elicited a flood of memories. His voice that she believed had been erased from her mind suddenly resurfaced. She heard not the singer's voice playing from her phone but the man who sang that love song to her so many months ago. Frozen in place with tears streaming down her cheeks, she reminisced about the night he held her and softly sang about his forever girl with the angel eyes.

The next day didn't bring any improvement. Her chest painfully tightened as her heart rate sped up and her stomach bottomed out because not ten feet from her was a walking image from the past. Doing a double take, she felt panic take hold of her before she could reassure herself that this person only had a similar appearance at first glance. It wasn't him. On the heels of this scare came disappointment that the stranger wasn't who she thought he was, which warred with relief and left profound confusion in its wake. The peace she had finally grasped was disrupted.

She scrambled to corral her chaotic thoughts and emotions to no avail for the tears reappeared the following day when she abruptly remembered an evening so precious to her. Before she knew it, she was back in his truck when he took her hand and brought it to his lips shortly before he murmured for the first time in person those three beautiful words. As she said it in return, he stroked his thumb across her lips and brought her face close to meet his for several heart-stopping kisses. She recalled the heady conversation after about when and how they fell in love, the palpable relief that the truth of the shift in their hearts was out in the open, and the excitement of that change that made leaving each other so difficult.

Through those days, she wondered how long it would take to move on and not be stuck in the past. Just as the days started shining brighter and her soul became a little more weightless, what she thought was no more struck once again. The past returned to take root in her thoughts, despondency crept back in, and grief pierced her bruised and battered heart once more.

She desperately wanted to banish the bittersweet memories, wayward thoughts, and painful emotions from her mind. She longed to permanently wipe away the evidence that her heart was once in his possession, yet those scars refused to fade away. Her soul ached to be loved for who she was and to truly love in return.

Through this recurrence of grief, she knew with absolute certainty that the one way out of this was to fall completely into the arms of Jesus. The void in her would only be filled by His presence, and His unparalleled love was what she actually craved. So she laid her burdens down once more at the feet of Jesus and chose surrender, knowing grace, peace, and true love could only be found there.

Waves of Pain

I was so mad at myself. I couldn't believe that, after doing so well for a while, I had taken a couple steps backwards in the moving-on process. The sheer panic and acute pain that ripped through me when I saw a man in a parking lot who looked eerily like my ex-boyfriend stunned me and left me shaking for over an hour. All of this the day after one of my Spotify playlists randomly threw in a song he had sung to me that transported me back in time to that evening. It threw me for a loop, and I was left floundering.

My text to one best friend was, "About had a panic attack because I saw someone that looked so much like you-know-who. My heart is still pounding."

My convo with my other best friend was more along the lines of, "I thought I had been doing good until I saw someone that looked just like him. Oh, and I heard 'our' song the other day and did not handle it well."

Even though I shared those struggles with them, I didn't tell either of them exactly how much it was affecting me. I didn't want anyone to know just how much I was hurting that week because I believed I was only being dramatic about it. So what did I do? I stuffed all the feelings and emotions, the struggles and the hurts, deep inside the dark crevices of my heart so they would remain untouched and forgotten. Instead of acknowledging and working through the pain, I buried it. Refused to let it control me. Denied that there was any more hurt to work through. Chalked it up to just being my emotional and stressed self.

A couple of weeks passed, and I thought I had gotten myself back under control. The business of life and getting ready to go on a trip distracted me from my random emotional low, but the distraction only allowed the pain to build up so much that I finally reached my breaking point. On vacation without my typical distractions, I could no longer ignore the unhealthy state in which I found myself. Everything in me escalated to where I finally just exploded. I soon found myself on vacation rushing out of my parents' Airbnb before my siblings witnessed my total emotional breakdown. During the hours of the night when the resort was peacefully quiet with nothing to disturb that tranquility, there I was sitting on a golf cart sobbing in my mom's arms. "I miss him so much. I'm so mad at myself because I thought I was doing better. Why can't I move on, Mom? Why does this hurt so badly?"

With tears in her voice, she responded, "You are doing so much better, and you will move on. The pain is going to come in waves. This is just a wave. You will get through this."

With time, I have found that to be true. The waves of pain from a storm that battered me and forced me to rebuild my life eventually slowed until one day, they stopped coming altogether. What was left of the wreckage in my heart was turned into something intricately more wonderful than what had previously stood in its place.

Stick with me as I share an analogy that brands me the residential contractor's daughter that I am. The life you build after a heartbreak is similar to rebuilding a house destroyed by a hurricane. You begin to clean up the disaster on the surface. Take out the trash, dry up the water, pick up what is visibly broken. But as time goes on, you find that there is damage you couldn't see at first. Rain begins to leak through the ceiling in the living room. Floors start to buckle up with water damage. The drywall in the bathroom looks like it's sagging from the weight of the water. You keep repairing what you see, but the destruction keeps revealing itself and compounding your frustrations. Before you know it, you're having to call in a contractor to replace the roof, put in new flooring, or even demolish the house to completely rebuild. The damages went much deeper than you initially expected, and while the rebuilding process was time-consuming, costly, and difficult, the end result brought welcome changes. Maybe you got that addition you always wanted to build or those floors were outdated anyways and it was time to replace. Either way, even though the storm rocked the house and destroyed it, the outcome was a beautiful, new house rebuilt on a stronger foundation that is better prepared for any other storm that may come.

Like the rebuilding process that happens in waves as the damages become visible, so are we when healing from heartbreak. It's messy. It's painful. You can make progress only to feel like you are taking steps back. But the heart that comes through the other side of the fire is so much stronger, resilient, and trusting in its Maker.

Healing through Community

We've already established that I'm an introvert who regularly attempts to hide what I'm truly feeling. I also absolutely hate crying in front of other people. I'm totally fine with comforting others who confide in me, but vice versa sends me running to the privacy of my house where I can be emotional all alone. Letting others in to glimpse what I'm thinking and feeling has just never come naturally for me.

Like I said earlier, after the first few days following the breakup, I closed myself off from others. I would share more details surrounding my relationship with my ex and talk a little bit with the people closest to me about what I was going through, but there was always a barrier. A wall I had carefully built around my heart surrounding the emotions dangerously close to the surface that threatened to break through at any moment. A fortress that guarded my already-crushed heart with no outside access, even to the people I love the most.

The walls we build up around our hearts look different for all of us, but for me, it meant not crying in front of and letting anyone know about my real emotions for almost five months.

I genuinely believed during that time frame that I was actually healing because I could discuss what happened without breaking down. I would applaud myself for keeping a tight rein on my tears and a peaceful veneer on my face in front of others. But in reality, instead of healing, the wound inside was becoming infected, spreading and consuming me. I didn't allow myself to have an outlet and severely underestimated the importance of community.

That night on vacation when I didn't have the strength left to continue hiding the grief and finally allowed myself to show the weak side to my parents and best friend was a turning point for me. Much more than I realized in the moment.

I think sometimes it's easier for us to encourage others than to allow others to encourage us. We want to appear strong and bulletproof and hate to show our weak spots. We tend to think we are being a burden if we let people lovingly care for us or annoying if we, God forbid, shed a tear or two when life becomes difficult.

In believing that we are becoming less self-focused if we never talk about our struggles, we miss some key points. The first being that we are really not moving the focus off of ourselves; if anything, we become more self-focused because we don't allow anyone to speak into our lives and offer wisdom and direction when needed, and we miss out on the power of praying community. In the name of humility, we become so intent on refusing to let others past the walls we build, but the spirit of pride is what is actually keeping us from doing so thanks to the mindset that tells us we can handle it on our own. The suck-it-up mindset.

The second thing we miss in not opening our lives up to trusted people is the beauty of encouraging others who may be going through something similar. Who knows if our stories will become the consoling inspiration they need to continue to push forward in their own story? What if it's the incentive they use to open up about their own lives as well? We also miss the resulting healing and freedom that come along with sharing with others what is on our hearts.

It's terrifying; trust me, I know. But the ensuing peace from being known is absolutely worth it.

In the fall after my breakup, my Bible study leader passed around a sign-up list for testimony sharing and one for snack duty. I initially only signed up to bring snacks one week in November because that was something I could definitely do, but testimony sharing? No, I'll pass. However, as a couple of weeks went by, I was increasingly beginning to feel that I should take a look at the other sign-up sheet again. I wrote my name on the list on a whim but thought I would either be able to get out of it or be able to share my story without a trace of emotion by the time November came around.

The week I signed up for came way too soon for my comfort, and I couldn't skip Bible study that week because that was the same week I was supposed to bring snacks for the group. Kicking myself for not thinking that through all the way, I showed up to Bible study with snacks and just prayed that everyone forgot I was signed up for testimony that night. Although I kept feeling that internal nudge (plus a friend of mine physically nudging me throughout Bible study), I was determined to ignore it because I thought my testimony wasn't important and nobody would want to listen to it. I also knew that I was still not at the point to where I could share my whole story without showing emotion.

Well, our Bible study leader did not forget who was signed up that night, so I did end up sharing my testimony at the end of our study that evening. I hated the way my voice immediately choked up and despised the tears that began to fall down my face halfway into it, but I made it through. When I finished, I looked at the women sitting around in our Bible study leader's living room and saw endless understanding and love. They not only selflessly listened to my choked-up, all-over-the-place story, but they also supported and encouraged me. They emboldened me with similar stories and shared advice, and I left that night feeling the weight that was sitting so heavily on my chest for over five months suddenly lift. I could finally breathe again.

Those two nights opening up to people in my life, as well as the day I finally forgave my ex-boyfriend and myself, were pivotal moments in my walk with Christ and recovering from the heartbreak. To be actually known by people in my life who truly cared for me was a healing balm to my heart. To be encouraged by others who had similar stories was comforting, and to allow the love of God to minister to me through the love shown by His Church was freeing and empowering.

"Bear one another's burden, and so fulfill the law of Christ" (Gal. 6:2 ESV).

"Encourage each other every day while you have the opportunity. If you do this, none of you will be deceived by sin and become stubborn" (Heb. 3:13 GW).

I've always thought of these verses in one way: Be the shoulder for others to cry on, but I had always seen it as a one-way street. Be the strong one. Don't be the weak one. Be the one others can come to with their burdens. But in that belief of mine, where was the allowance for me to share my burdens? Who was going to be the strong shoulder that I can lean on when life pulled me into the pits? It can be easy to realize the instruction Paul gave to the Galatians to be a good, loving friend to others, but sometimes, we can be so focused on doing what looks to be the right thing that we miss the second, lesser taught instruction wrapped up in the same verse. Let others be good, loving friends to you as well.

It is a hit to your pride to allow others to see your struggles and weaknesses, but this is where we lift each other up, admonish each other if need be, and thrive in God-given community. None of us were created to live isolated and self-sufficient. We need the strength and salvation of Jesus and the community and closeness with other believers who can encourage and love us through our lows.

Perspective Change

If you grew up in a Christian environment or have been studying the Bible for long, you probably know of the story of Lot and his family escaping Sodom and Gomorrah as the cities were destroyed (Gen. 19:1–29). You most likely also know of the pillar of salt that Lot's wife was turned into as she looked behind her after being strictly told to not do so.

Growing up, I've always wondered why it was so wrong for his wife to look back and why that necessitated such a drastic outcome. If I saw fire falling from heaven, I know I would want a glimpse because that's not something you see every day. I would imagine it was still somewhat dark as it was in the early morning, so to see the dawn hours being suddenly lit up by the raining fire pelting the cities with a fierce intensity and leaving sheer chaos in its wake, all due to a considerably evil environment, would probably be remarkable to witness because of its testament to God's amazing power. At least from a safe distance.

In Genesis 19:15, we see that the angels are urging Lot to take his family and flee Sodom. They had just witnessed the sickening acts of the men of Sodom, and the angels subsequently filled Lot in on God's plan to completely destroy the cities because of the wickedness. Even after being told by angels sent from God that the city he was living in was about to be demolished, we read in verse 16 that Lot hesitated. He lingered in leaving Sodom. So what did the angels have to do? They forced him and his family out because of God's mercy toward them and commanded them to not look back to Sodom. Fast forward to verse 26 where his wife disobeys and is then turned into salt.

So how did a seemingly innocent glance over her shoulder translate into Lot's wife being turned into a pillar of salt? It could be that it wasn't the actual physical glance back to Sodom that condemned her but the desire to return to the place from which she was just delivered.

You may be asking why I would put the story of Lot and his wife in a book about breakups and heartache. Two very different situations, yes, but one common thread of God's purpose for us in moving from the past.

In studying this story, I've noticed a few key points that, although indescribably more severe than a breakup, are still relevant to us today. Like Lot, we can find ourselves in situations that are ultimately not the best for us and do not highlight Christ living in us. Living in that city was not exactly a healthy environment for someone trying to live a godly life just as some relationships we have may not be encouraging in our walks with Christ. Because of social pressures and consistent stress, we can begin to lower our standards and not realize the negative effects this has on ourselves and the people around us (Lot was going to give his daughters to the men outside his door; it can't get much lower than that). Because of God's mercy and desire to see us with fruitful, thriving lives, sometimes He can forcefully remove us from these situations for our own good and His glory (the angels gave Lot no choice but to leave Sodom).

But there are times when our hearts are so intertwined with the person we loved or the situation we thought we found happiness in, that our souls long to return to that place. That was where Lot's wife went wrong. It wasn't the actual glance back to see the cities being destroyed. It was the craving to go back to that old way of life. It was the distrust that God had something so much better than what she could imagine. It was the refusal to accept His gift of freedom from that life because her cloudy perspective only allowed her to see what she was missing instead of what she was gaining.

I know how difficult and painful that perspective shift can be because it's natural to only see in the moment what is being taken from you. There's a massive part of your life that has just been ripped away and all you can see is the gaping hole left behind. Every breath hurts as you fight against the desire of running back to that person you loved or that life you lived. The false sense of comfort and security that's suddenly missing leaves you wondering if there will ever be another safe place to exist for you. There's an ache in your neck from continually glancing back over your shoulder to the past; the present is obscure and the future is uncertain because you're turned the opposite way still living in days gone by.

In the seven months following my breakup, I was constantly living with a mindset that I needed to forget him and forget the memories we made together. Some memories affected me worse than others, but with each one, I would always be disappointed and angry with myself for thinking about him again. I thought that in order to move on, I had to forget everything, so when another day would go by and I thought of him again, I would be discouraged that I wasn't healing and that I was still hung up on him. I hated the unbidden flashbacks that daily life provoked and hated myself for not succeeding in banishing him from my mind and for the lingering effects I allowed him to have on my heart. I'd pray that I would just forget everything and then be mad when God didn't hit the factory reset button on my brain. I was measuring progress by how many times

I thought back on memories instead of realizing the actual healing work God was doing in me.

I can't tell you how it happened other than that it was the grace of God, but I finally came to a point where I understood that the memories aren't bad to have. No matter how much I may want to, I can't just erase everything that happened. Sure, I could delete our pictures from Instagram and my camera roll, but there was no possible way to eliminate them from my mind. Instead of trying to program myself to not think about the past, I had to learn to not *dwell* on it or *desire* to live in those days again.

I had finally come to realize that healing from a broken heart doesn't mean forgetting the past because that can't be done. Instead, it comes from taking the past and what has been done to you or by you and finding the lessons to be learned and using them as a source of comfort and encouragement for yourself and others.

Learning to shift your perspective from one of longing for the past to one of gratitude that it happened and renewed purpose in living in the present takes hard work. Moving from missing that person so much you become sick to thinking back to those memories with some level of fondness for the fun times and reflection on the lessons learned, yet with a certain detachment, takes time. Filling the excruciating void left in your heart takes only Jesus, and finding forgiveness for them and for yourself ultimately takes a choice and drawn strength from the One who has forgiven you.

I Forgive You

The time in between dreams of him began to increase. He may have been in the latest dream, but this time was different. This time, she felt herself emotionally pull away from him because of the way he had hurt her again. Even in this foggy fantasy her mind played during deep slumber, she began to see more clearly his true character and subconsciously distanced herself more.

During the waking moments, the lingering feeling of his arms around her started to lessen and the taste of his lips a faint memory. She could barely recall the deep timbre of his voice or the contagious laugh that used to make her heart melt. The picture of his smile seemed a little more pixelated with each day, and his presence in her mind began to recede.

She belatedly noticed the anniversaries of important events, and the dates she feared would serve as a painful reminder of what she lost slowly became just ordinary days. Time sped by regardless of whether she was ready for it or not.

With this gradual freedom came relief and healing but also sadness that she was moving on from the one she had loved. A small piece of her wanted to hang tightly to the past, to battle against the diminishing feelings and memories, but a larger part was experiencing the blooming hope of a wonderful, bright tomorrow.

The Keys to My Heart

Remember a few chapters back when I said that there was a repeated situation right before the breakup that left me pretty wounded and the fears I shared with him were casually brushed off? I've decided I'm going to share some of those details, but before I do that, I need to back up some to childhood.

As an Enneagram 9, my core fear is losing relationships with people I love. I take these personality tests with a grain of salt, but that one hit the nail right on the head. I think we can all say we fear losing loved ones to death, but with my personality and the way I crave stability and peace in relationships, this fear is heightened. Add in the possibility of someone walking out on me in life? Terrifying.

Growing up, I was blessed with a godly, stable home. It's something I strive not to take for granted. I was raised by loving parents in a healthy, happy marriage and was surrounded by family on all sides. Life wasn't perfect by any means, but it was great. However, there was always a lingering fear and an overwhelming anxiety of the people I love being taken from me.

Many of my friends in my childhood came from broken homes. I saw the devastation left behind by divorce and abandonment or death and grief, and I was scared it would happen to my family. I believe that in this broken world we live in these fears can be reasonable to a degree. But when they keep you up at night as a child at six years old, replaying and dwelling on the scares of almost losing your dad to pneumonia months past it happening or stuck in a constant state of fearing the worst possible scenario when your mom goes through a rough pregnancy, that's when it becomes too much. When you can't sleep for worry that your parents will get a divorce after a minor argument just because your friend's parents split is unreasonable and the fear groundless. Worrying that every little thing you say or do will destroy the friendships you value keeps you walking on eggshells. When you take on the emotions of the people around you just to keep a sense of stability and harmony so as not to risk pushing them away from you and losing your connection with them, there's an internal, spiritual issue that needs to be addressed. And that fearful person was me for a very long time.

As I got older, the fear of my parents ever getting divorced went away (I came to realize and truly believe that "divorce" was not in their vocabulary), but the fear of me having broken relationships or losing loved ones through death never went away. If I thought too much about it, I would actually start to panic. Although I've been able to handle this better through only the grace of God, it was still something I would struggle with surrendering completely to God. This brings us to the week before my breakup.

After I had fallen in love with my ex-boyfriend, I had quickly gotten to the point where I couldn't sleep if we didn't talk beforehand. Whether it was by phone call or text, it was our ritual to always say, "Goodnight, babe. I love you." No matter what. I needed to know, especially because of the nature of his job, that he was safe and well and that our relationship was on steady ground. When my text was left unanswered one night, I figured he probably thought he texted back but it didn't send. That happens. Regardless, it was a sleepless night for me because my brain ran through every scenario. Did he get sick? Was he called into work for an emergency, and if so, was it a dangerous situation he was called into? Did I make him upset? Is he just getting annoyed with me? All these questions swirled in my mind through the long hours of the night. The morning came, he confirmed that he thought he texted back but didn't send it, and we went on our way. The next night, it happened again. This time, I knew it could not have been an oversight, and I was livid. I was already exhausted from not sleeping because of the first incident. Now I had to go through a second night of absolutely no sleep because he couldn't send one text to or press one button to call his girlfriend? After all of our other problems we were having, now this?

Once 1:00 a.m. rolled around and I was wide awake and anxious, I decided to distract myself with social media. I logged in to see that my boyfriend was active on Facebook Messenger. *Um, excuse me? What? Apparently, messaging people on Facebook took priority over reassuring me?* I immediately texted him, "We need to talk in the morning." There was more to the message than that, but that was the gist of it. I was angry with him, hurt, and exhausted, but I immediately felt so guilty when he texted back right away saying that he never received my text. I knew he was irritated with me, and I felt like a fool for getting upset over a text message or lack thereof.

The next day, I tried my best to cool down and logically think through everything. I had already apologized to him a couple of times for getting upset about what had happened, but I felt like I needed to explain more of the why behind my reaction. Not to justify myself but to help him get a glimpse into how my brain works. I know now that I'm not at fault for what happened; I got more information later about what he was doing and why he didn't text back, so my reaction actually was logical and justified. But at that time, I didn't feel like it was and thought I was becoming too much and was pushing him away.

That evening, I psyched myself up for sharing about my fears that have been a lifelong struggle. After warning him in advance that I might get emotional and that I've never actually shared this in-depth with anyone, I called him and told him that the reason for my reaction was that I'm scared to lose the people I love. I hold on too tightly and can read into things which led to panic that he was slipping from me. I'm scared of being walked out on. Terrified of losing him which is why I freaked out when I thought something had happened to him on his work trip weeks prior. With those hated tears making my voice shake while barely getting those words spoken without full-on sobbing, I waited for his response. "I didn't know you were that upset" drifted across the line in the most casual, unconcerned tone. And that was the end of that conversation. Nothing more was said on the matter. And our phone call, the last one we would ever have, lasted maybe five more minutes after that.

His response was painfully cold and callous to me. I felt as if I was stupid and dramatic for feeling as I did, and for months after that, I regretted ever being vulnerable and sharing things I had never spoken aloud before. I thought sharing what I did would bring us closer and make our relationship stronger because more walls were being torn down. Instead of stewing in my anxiety and expecting him to just magically know how I was feeling, I decided to tell him. I chose to tear down that last emotional barrier I kept carefully built around my heart and to let him fully in, knowing I was handing him the power to do whatever he wanted with the unrestrained access to my heart.

So you can imagine the betrayal I felt when he left me just days after that conversation in the way that he did. I felt as if my decision to be vulnerable backfired because, before I knew it, I was living out my worst fear.

Along with my grief of the man I loved walking out on me, the betrayal of him taking my fears and breaking up with me in one of the worst ways possible, and the gaping wound left behind, I struggled with the lack of closure. There wasn't a big fight with arguments and yelling. No explanation of the sudden coldness coming my way for the last two weeks of our relationship. Nothing to clue me in on the abrupt change in his "love" for me. All I was left with was the startling reality of his true character and imagined scenarios of the missing parts of his life I had been lied to about.

After the breakup, I was able to put a few of the pieces together in what had most likely happened with him over those weeks, but there were still so many parts for which I was left in the dark. I was going crazy attempting to fill in the missing gaps by analyzing everything repeatedly and trying to decide what to say and ask if I were to ever get the chance of speaking to him again. I was able to ease up over time on constantly trying to piece together what happened, but there was still a part of me that wanted to find out the truth from him.

Throughout those months, I would find myself worrying about him, continuously thinking of him, and the anger I had toward his actions would fade quickly each time it was resurrected. Because I knew I didn't hate him, I believed I had come to a point of forgiveness, but constantly dwelling on the past and the what-ifs and should-have-beens said otherwise. Imagined responses if a chance meeting were to happen formed in my head, and I still lived each day with bated breath and a slight hope that there would be some form of closure to come. I would pray for him and pray that he would change and become a better man, not only for himself and his relationship with Jesus, but also for whoever his future wife would be. But immediately after speaking those words, I would feel like I was going to be sick and then spend the next hour calming myself down from the panic and anger the thought of him with another woman induced. Deep down, I prayed for his change only so that he would come back one day, and we could finally become what I had prayed we would be.

I was still holding on so tightly to him and still allowed him to have such a powerful control over me that I knew that what I had thought to be forgiveness was actually only hallow words spoken out of mere obligation instead of sincerity.

No Strings Attached

After that night on vacation when I finally let others past the wall I had put up, I had to process the pain and deal with the grief once more. I took an extended break from writing this book to heal more and come to a better place emotionally. Processing the pain this time, however, was different. Because of the encouragement and love from my people, I was able to have a different outlook. My outlook this time around was one of patience with myself, full reliance on the Lord, and opening my heart up to the people closest to me. I dove headfirst into spending time with my Savior and living in His love instead of sitting in the ashes of a failed love, and in doing that, I was able to see what He needed me to do.

I needed to choose forgiveness.

I had to come to an understanding that forgiveness is not holding onto the past, whether that is by purposefully replaying memories or hanging onto physical mementos. It is not waiting by the phone hoping for that out-of-area number to light up the screen and praying you'd hear that voice on the other line begging for another chance. It is not the absence of negative emotions but the choice to not stew in them and to instead allow them to work in you for a positive change. Forgiveness is not remaining bitter, either to the person who hurt you or toward yourself. Forgiveness is not obliging the deep hurts and wounds to form a callous so thick around your heart that you become resentful toward the future but allowing your heart to soften once more.

Two weeks later, I was able to come to a new point of surrender and true forgiveness. Over that time, I had begun to feel more of an ability to forgive with no strings attached, an ability only provided through the strength of Jesus and only found through prioritizing Him as first in my life, letting Him work in me, and accepting His forgiveness for myself. I began to feel the beginning stirrings of a new freedom in my soul and knew it was time to actually surrender everything.

I best process my thoughts through writing, so I sat down on my couch late one night and finally put my real thoughts and feelings to paper. I've debated whether or not to include the following. While my other writings are just as real, this one is significantly more raw, vulnerable, and personal. I wrote this as if I was writing a letter to my ex, never to be seen by him. But if this helps one person take steps toward forgiveness, then I think this is worth sharing.

> *As much as I may have wanted to, I couldn't hate you. In those tortuous middle-of-the-night hours when sobs wracked my body and depression darkened the door of my heart, it was impossible to truly wish the depths of that pain on you.*
>
> *Bitterness toward the ideals of love and trust began to swell, but toward you, there was none. Anger for the way you lied and discarded me was present, but antipathy for you was strangely absent.*
>
> *Admittedly, for a long while, I didn't want you to move on. Thoughts of you in the arms of someone else were like repeated knife thrusts into my heart. I didn't wish for you to be in the turmoil I was experiencing, but neither did I desire for you to give up on me so easily. Without a backward glance or a second thought.*
>
> *I wondered if hating you would have been easier than slowly and painfully extricating myself from my love for you. Maybe it would have been simpler to hold animosity toward you, but if I did, I wouldn't be where I am today.*

Today, I am free in my rediscovered identity in Christ. I am no longer bound in chains by our turbulent past or our thwarted, once-imagined future. Because of those long, miserable months, my faith has grown more than I thought possible.

Although you left me utterly broken, you showed me that I could open up my heart. Because of that and despite ours being a wrong and destructive love, I can now know that with the right man I will love deeper and stronger than I can even imagine. With the right man, a love that is godly and selfless will be infinitely more beautiful than what I ever thought we had.

Even though you were wrong for me and I for you, you were the man God ultimately used to change me for the better through the heartbreak and lessons learned.

The road has been long and arduous, but I believe I have finally come to the place where I can say this without hesitation or pretense:

I forgive you.

Forgiving What Can't Be Forgotten

The human heart feels deeply; that's just how we were created. As with our physical body, we receive bruises, cuts, and scars emotionally. Words are spoken that wound, people walk out and leave behind trust issues, events happen that shake your world. Major life events leave you overcome and small disappointments accumulate over time to result in thick scars. It's a part of life. It's a part of the broken world we live in. On this side of eternity, there's no escaping it. It's discouraging, but there is some good news.

We have this hope that changes everything.

There's this beautiful hope that we can cling tightly to, a confidence that one day all tears and all pain will be wiped away. There will come a day when we no longer have to process grief and heal trauma. Disappointments will no more hold us back, and chaos will end. There is going to be a day when we see the most perfect love in all its glory and we will cease to remember the times on earth where love was treated as no more than a game to be played, an upper hand to be had. There will come a day when we will sing and dance in worship to our King without the temptation of stress and anxiety pulling us away. One day soon, we will enter a time of the purest joy, living in beautiful abandon under the wings of the Most High. There will come a day when Jesus returns in all His majesty to usher in His kingdom, but until that day, how do we walk through this broken life without being overcome with the worries and difficulties of this world?

We live out His kingdom on earth.

As God's children, redeemed and forgiven (Eph. 2:8), we are given the freedom and ability to love as Jesus loved and to walk through life as He did. He commissioned His people to go out and make disciples and to live a life so radically different from the world that others will have no choice but to see Jesus in us. And what is the ultimate example of this? Keeping the two greatest commandments: (1) Love God with all your heart, soul, and mind and (2) Love your neighbor as yourself.

This love we're to have doesn't mean we have to feel a certain type of way; it's a choice. It doesn't exclude the other instructions in the Bible; it encompasses all the commands in that they are all about either loving God or loving others. This love doesn't mean life is all sunshine and roses and we're to keep a cheerful smile plastered on our face at all times, but it does mean doing the hard work to press on and trust God when life is hard and to selflessly serve those around us and be the hands and feet of Jesus. The greatest example of this love may be the hardest because it also means *forgiving what can't be forgotten.*

At this point, you may be thinking, *They don't deserve forgiveness. What they did was terribly wrong and I will never be able to forget that. They haven't even asked for forgiveness!* And to that, I will say you're absolutely right. They don't deserve forgiveness. But let me share something else in the most gentle, loving way possible.

Neither do we deserve forgiveness.

Every person has a story of pain and wrong done to them, and each story is different and unique. I don't know your story and what has deeply hurt you, shaken your world, and left you with unanswered questions and unhealed wounds. I do know that what was done was wrong, and I'm so sorry you had to walk through that. No matter what type of pain you've had to cope with, do not minimize it. At the same time, keep in perspective the most horrific wrong to ever be committed and the result of that horrendous act.

We serve a perfect God who cannot abide with sin (Ps. 5:4), yet He loved us so much (John 3:16) that He would come as a perfect human who was tempted just as we are yet never sinned Himself (Heb. 4:15) to provide a way of salvation for us (John 14:6), even though we are sinful by nature (Rom. 3:23), so that we can be called children of God (John 1:12) and be given the gift and promise of eternal life with Him (Rom. 6:23). He was betrayed, beaten, pierced, persecuted, spit on, humiliated, abandoned by those who claimed to love Him, hung on a cross with nails driven into His hands and feet, and died the most gruesome death at the hands of the people He came to save. The people He loved. Yet as Jesus hung on that cross and looked out on the undeserving faces of those who tortured and mocked Him, He did the unthinkable.

"Father, forgive them, for they do not know what they do" (Luke 23:34).

How incredible to know that there is a love so pure, so strong, and so forgiving and that our Lord would go through such great lengths to be able to make us His own. From the minute Adam and Eve ate of that forbidden fruit to this very moment, we have sinned countless times and turned our back on Him. Every time we sin, we are essentially putting Him back on that cross. He went through the worst heartbreak imaginable, yet He still chooses to forgive. He still gives the undeserved mercy we receive when we accept Him as our Savior, and He continues to welcome us back with open arms every single time we mess up. This perfect and selfless act of forgiveness and mercy should spur us on to extend forgiveness to those who also don't deserve it. Because the truth is, we don't deserve it either. There is no sin too big or too small that He can't forgive (1 John 1:9), and through the power freely given by the Holy Spirit, we too can have that ability to forgive as He has forgiven us.

So how do we forgive? When should we forgive? And how do we keep choosing forgiveness?

We can only forgive when we accept forgiveness from God. If we haven't chosen to accept forgiveness for ourselves, how can we extend it to others? When we allow the forgiveness of God to permeate our souls, we are set free from the weight of our own mistakes and the ways we have hurt others. Our own guilt no longer is a weight around our neck that pulls us down deeper and deeper with each new painful situation and each mistake we make. Instead, it becomes what spurs us on toward uncharted growth and instills in us the ability to forgive others.

After allowing the mercy of God to seep into the hidden places of our souls and bring light to the shadows, accepting forgiveness for what we have done, we must acknowledge what has been done to us. Even when it's difficult and all we desire is to stuff the pain deep down, we must confront the hurts head-on. We have to face what has wounded us. We need to acknowledge what has been taken and the impact the actions of others have had on us. There is no forgiveness where there is no acknowledgment of the depth of the wrongs. If we stay in denial about the extent of our hurts, they will eventually come to a head in the most inconvenient way at the worst time. Don't diminish the pain. Don't bury it under mounds of dismissal and downplay. Allow the sorrow and grief to run its course.

But then…Oh, there always has to be a *but then,* huh? But then, we have to pick ourselves up, dust ourselves off, and begin to move forward. However, none of this can be done without forgiving those who pushed us to the pit of pain in which we find ourselves. Forgiveness is the release of the need for revenge and the desire to see them hurt as much as you. It's letting go of the power they have over you and instead handing those reins to the Father. It's surrendering the loss that carved a hole inside a once-whole heart, the dreams crushed beyond words, the need for control of present and future situations, the panic and grief and depression. It's surrendering it all to the more-than-capable hands of Jesus and letting Him continue to write the story of your life.

It's simply said but not-so-simply done. It takes time. It takes grace. It takes the power of Jesus. How long it takes for one person to heal is not how long it will take another person. There is no easy answer to when you should be able to forgive, but I will say this. Working toward forgiveness starts the very minute someone does you wrong. It's a process that is fraught with pain. But it's a hard road worth walking as it means freedom from the enslavement of bitterness and the ability to move forward in life without being chained to sit in the ugly ashes of the past.

It Isn't What You Think It Is

Forgiveness is not a one-and-done deal.

At least not most of the time. After that moment of true forgiveness I talked about earlier, I've had to continually choose to forgive my ex when the hurts and insecurities rear their ugly heads. When suspicions arise and more pieces of the story fall into place, I have to choose to let go of my resentment toward the others who were negatively involved and remind myself the choices he made were his alone. I have to allow forgiveness to soften my heart when the baggage I've carried weighs me down and hardens me. When the disgust and hate with myself come into play, I have to let go of the desire for perfectionism and need for control. Forgiveness is a daily choice. It's what you have to choose when the old wounds resurface. Forgiveness is not something we can master and turn on with the flip of a switch but is a constant battle we fight that, thankfully, is already won through the power of Jesus.

In Matthew 18:21–22, Jesus blew the idea of forgiveness out of the water when His disciples questioned Him about it. In that time, Jewish culture taught that only God can forgive sins and forgiving each other was a foreign concept, even blasphemy (see Luke 5:21). Forgiveness was only attainable through the sacrificial system of the day. So can you imagine what Peter was feeling when he shared what he probably thought to be a ground-breaking moral of that day? "Then Peter came to Jesus and asked, 'Lord, how many times shall I forgive my brother or sister who sins against me? Up to seven times?'" (Matt. 18:21). Even today, we can look at that and think, *Yeah, seven seems impossible. Forgiving once is pushing it.*

But Jesus knew then what we know now through His written Word. Through the power His forgiveness of our sins has given us, we can forgive, *not seven times, but seventy-seven times* (Matt. 18:22). This indicates that He wants us to continue to forgive those who hurt us, not to reach a certain number and then call it quits, but to keep choosing the forgiveness even when they keep hurting us. Even when the same hurts are resurrected. We don't stop forgiving because He has not stopped forgiving us.

Forgiveness is not forgetting.

You can't make yourself forget an event that has traumatized you, destroyed your trust, and shaped your life. There's no way to just blot out the pain. There is no delete button in the brain for the files upon files of hurts, trauma, and memories. Goodness, I wish there was. I truly wish there was a way to put a hard stop to the triggers that bring flashbacks of both the good and bad and that bring that cursed ache back to the surface. But there is a bright side to not being able to forget. You remember things that help you avoid similar situations. You learn more about yourself and you grow.

While forgetting may not be possible, the presence of the pain and memories do begin to fade. Sometimes, it's a noticeable difference. Other times, it's gradual. For me, the dreams I would have of my ex every night started to fade very slowly months after the breakup, but when I was able to truly forgive and chose to daily surrender my hurts, broken dreams, and desires, the dreams went from multiple times a week to maybe once every other week. As time went on, they happened very rarely. And today, I can't remember when was the last time I dreamed of him because it's been that long ago. Other reminders and triggers also became less painful. Important days that

I believed would be pure torture became easier to walk through with the passing of each day.

I know it's discouraging when the past keeps resurfacing and the wounds keep reopening, but the more you choose forgiveness and the more you fall into the gracious arms of Jesus, the more you heal. And before you know it, you begin to see the beauty in life again. The days start shining a little brighter with the rays of renewed hope, and the nights don't seem as daunting as the blackness outside no longer matches the darkness that once resided in your heart. You may not be completely free from the memories, but you can be completely free from the effect those memories once had on you. You *can* choose to let them go.

Forgiveness does not always mean reconciliation.

There are instances, of course, where restoring a relationship is possible, but this does not mean that it should happen with everybody. Some relationships are best left in the past to rest in peace. Boundaries are good and healthy for all people involved. Do not let anybody guilt you into tearing down those boundaries in the name of forgiveness because oftentimes, forgiveness is more easily attained with distance. Unless there has been a sincere change of heart that is backed by long-term evidence, some relationships should not be restored. It is not loving to keep allowing those who have repeatedly crushed your heart to continually have access. Boundaries *are* loving.

Guarding our hearts oftentimes looks like setting up guardrails that do not allow easy access to those who will harm us. This doesn't mean we stay closed off to everyone around us but that we be wise in who we let into the deepest parts of our hearts.

Learning to Walk Again

Little does he know that the way he destroyed her changed her for the better. He doesn't realize that the heart he broke is being built back stronger. His duplicitous love only served to make her seek the unfailing, trustworthy love of Jesus while the steadfastness and faithfulness of God were highlighted by his immaturity and unwillingness to commit. The raging storm in her heart he left for her to weather alone was the chance for her to see her Savior walk on water and lift her from treacherous waves. He doesn't know that he is becoming her past more with every day.

While the past is unaware of the present and future, the future is equally incognizant of the past.

Little does he know that when he meets her, her shyness and hesitation are just as much due to former experiences as they are her personality. She will question everything and be slow to trust and fall for him, but as of now, he is oblivious to this. He isn't thinking that she's now gun-shy with love and will need additional patience and reassurance, but what he should know is that her heart is on lockdown and he can only gain access through Jesus. Little does he know that when she finally opens herself up to him, she will be all in and she will be able to say that he was worth the wait.

Ghosted

It was Wednesday night Bible study again, and during the beginning when we each shared our highs and lows of the week, I was excited to share my unique, somewhat weird (okay, very weird) high. *So, my high of the week is that a guy I was talking to ghosted me. What can I say? It's the little things that make me happy.*

I should probably explain the strange elation that came with this turn of events. The very next night after I forgave my ex-boyfriend, a stranger slid into my DMs. His opening line was funny, and without thinking, I decided to message back and give it a go. I thought my sarcasm would send him running, but it didn't. At least not right away. Once the implications of what I was doing hit me, there was so much hesitation in continuing a conversation with him because of the fear I had of dating again. But it wasn't crippling. I knew I was going to have to face this sooner or later. It felt possible this time around and so much different than the time two months prior when I had thought of dating again. The time I had a full-on panic attack…

Let's go back a couple of months in time.

Almost two months before this, I had gone to a conference and met a guy who my cousin swore was interested in me. I didn't see any indications of interest, but she shared with me what she picked up from the parts of our conversation she heard. I still didn't see any interest from him myself, but I still freaked out. And definitely not in a good way. I laid wide awake that night in full-blown panic as I thought of what I would do if there was a chance of him being interested in me. I was terrified, and the thought of getting to know a new guy seemed impossible for me. All I could think about was my ex, and I knew without a doubt that I was nowhere close to being able to date again. For crying out loud, I froze the first day at the conference because there was a man in front of me in the check-in line who looked more like my ex than his own brothers did! It was discouraging, and I was angry at myself for being this way. With dread, I walked into the second day of the conference and prayed I wouldn't run into this man who supposedly was "interested" in me and that we wouldn't see each other in the confusing throng of thousands of people. My heart started beating wildly, and I was having trouble breathing walking into those doors; I was already thinking through a response to let him down just in case he was interested. Crazy, right? But the thought process my panic led me into was anything but reasonable. I significantly relaxed when I didn't see him, and nothing came out of that conversation with the stranger at the conference. Even though it had been a few months since my past relationship ended, it was apparently still too fresh to even think about new possibilities again. I knew, without a doubt, that I was not ready to jump back into the dating scene again.

I was still too wrapped up in a past love to consider any future love. Thinking about the fact that I would have to open myself up again and enter into another relationship one day crippled me. I was terrified. And on my flight home after the conference, I struggled with the fears of having to learn to love once more. It just didn't seem possible for me at that moment. My heart screamed at me that it wasn't right each time I thought about putting myself out there once more. It was as if my heart was telling me that considering a future with someone new wouldn't be faithful because I was still clinging to the last threads of a love ripped away. Some part of me was still very much encased in the past, and it seemed I would never be able to break free from those chains. But with time, I found myself slowly releasing the death grip I had on what remained of that unrequited, fatal love. One by one, those threads gradually disintegrated and I slowly felt freer to move forward in life.

That's why being ghosted by the guy who slid into my DMs was a victory for me in a sense. I didn't exactly want to enter into another relationship, but I also knew there would be no harm in talking to this guy and possibly giving him the first date he asked me on. Who knew what it could turn into? I was willing to give it just one chance. He ghosted me after asking me out, so we never went on that date. A series of events showed that dating him would've been a mistake because of his character that started to show, but I was thankful that in talking to him for that short amount of time, I was able to do so without being consumed with thoughts of my ex and missing him and what we had. It seems small, but it was a victory for me. Even though things didn't work out with the stranger in my DMs, in the long run I was slowly, oh so slowly, gaining hope that I would be able to fully move on from the man I had once loved.

Sparks Fly

As the months crept by, I still found myself with some fears. Sure, I was finally able to entertain the potential of another relationship without being consumed by memories of my ex-boyfriend, but there was no interest on my side in talking to the guys who seemed to be interested in me. *Was there something wrong with me?* I just was not attracted to them at all. Would I always compare a new guy to a man I no longer had? Would I always look at and talk to him and feel absolutely nothing? That lie of never being able to love again began to creep back in my heart as doubts of whether or not I would ever find another guy with that same chemistry I once had with my ex swirled around my mind.

Time passed, and more people came into my life. And still, there was nobody that caught my attention. While part of me was happy that I wasn't getting swept up into feelings for somebody new and that I could focus solely on my relationship with Christ, I was still worried that I might not ever find another guy with whom that chemistry existed. Honestly, it seemed like I was numb inside. I felt as if a part of me had died when I walked away from the mirage of a future with the only man I had loved up to that point in my life, and nobody seemed to be able to resurrect those feelings within me.

And then there were all the messages from Christian speakers I was listening to who said that chemistry and attraction are not priority. A mindset that is becoming more common in Christian culture began to warp my mind. *Give every Christian guy a chance no matter if you're attracted to them or not.* I would take that and try to make myself be open to dating any godly man, but I just couldn't. What I was failing to realize was that it *does* hold some importance. Chemistry is not the most important aspect of a relationship, and attraction is not the sole basis for love. If it was, the relationship would be over as soon as it started. But there *definitely* should be value of chemistry in a relationship. Some may hold to that exact statement about dating regardless of attraction, but it hasn't felt accurate to me. While there are times when attraction is not felt right away and comes later down the road, my personal opinion is that a relationship should start with some level of attraction.

What I've come to realize is that every person finds different people attractive. *And that's okay.* I don't believe there is something inherently wrong with finding a certain look more attractive than another. Girls, if you find yourself more drawn to the tall guys with the dark looks or you guys find yourself more attracted to the short blondes, there is no shame in that. Or if you are more attracted to reserved introverts or bubbly extroverts, that's not wrong either. That's how God made us. He made us all differently and beautifully. And while each and every person is wonderfully made and uniquely beautiful, some of us may be created to feel that chemistry with only certain kinds of people.

With that in mind, I began to stop berating myself for not finding new guys attractive. Just because I wasn't feeling that "spark" with guys I met did not mean that I was still hung up on attraction to my ex. So I continued with life and continued with meeting new people. But then I was completely thrown off guard when one day, the chemistry and attraction I thought I would never feel again hit me full force. When at one moment I couldn't fathom experiencing any of that again, the very next I was proved wrong. It was exciting.

But if I'm being completely transparent, it was also terrifying.

With my attraction to this guy, there came a certain vulnerability that I haven't had to face in quiet some time. It's nerve-racking to put yourself back out there and risk rejection and heartbreak again. To open yourself up once more to the possibility of a new relationship and potential love is intimidating. It can feel as if you're prying open the doors of your heart and struggling against the weight of fear pushing back against you.

This time, however, was different for me because I was so much more secure in my identity in Christ. Yes, it was scary to find myself with feelings for someone new, but this time I had more confidence and trust that, in Jesus, I would be completely fine. I was able to enter dating again with the mindset of, *If it works, then great. Praise God. But if it doesn't, then the love of my Savior will anchor me once again and I will still be able to praise God.*

Even through the fears and excitement of feeling that spark with someone again, I found myself immensely grateful for how the timing had played out. Because I had been so in love and began to imagine and plan a future with my ex, I didn't want to rebound. I didn't want to enter into another relationship if I wasn't healed from the last. So the many months between breaking up and finding myself attracted to a new guy gave me confidence that this wasn't a rebound, and all the thoughts of, *What is wrong me with for not finding new guys attractive*, became no more.

All of that to say, if you are in the same boat I was in, imagining a future with someone new feeling completely foreign and impossible, it does eventually change. You will find another person you will feel that same spark and connection with, maybe more so, and you will be able to move from that attraction and chemistry to building a beautiful relationship if that's what God has in store for you. One day, there will no longer be any more pull from a past love that keeps you from moving forward, and with time, you will find that your heart once again has room for someone new to enter.

Jumping Off the Diving Board

When I was five, I was invited to a friend's birthday party. He and his family had just moved into a house with a pool, so the invitation included bringing a swimsuit and a plan to enjoy the day in the sun. There was a problem though. I didn't know how to swim. I wasn't going to make myself look like the weird kid with floaties in a group full of kids who were avid swimmers, so I ditched the additional, much-needed help and decided to just stick to the shallow end. That lasted a few minutes until I saw my friends move to the deep end to do tricks off the diving board. So you can imagine how much my little five-year-old self started to feel FOMO when I saw them move to the opposite end of the pool. I began to ease myself along the edge, slowly creeping forward and making sure my feet were still touching the concrete bottom of the pool. *This isn't so bad. As long as I keep a hold of the wall, I'll be safe and be able to join in on the fun.* Every inch bolstered my courage. It seemed to me that there was nothing to swimming. I felt like I had mastered it because I was getting closer and closer to the end goal without mishap. I was confident in what I was doing and knew where I was going. There was nothing to stop me.

Until one inch made all the difference and before I knew it, I found myself missing the comforting presence of the wall and the concrete under my feet, fighting to break the surface. I *didn't* know how to swim. And I was drowning.

I don't remember much more after that other than my mom diving in to save me. The rest of the day was a blur as I fought a newfound fear of water. *I won't ever get in a pool again.* But my plans of never swimming again apparently did not line up with my mom's plans because she put me in swimming lessons before I could catch my breath.

As my adult life has moved on, I've had some déjà vu moments, making me feel like I'm learning to swim for the first time as a child after almost drowning. My first tentative step into dating again felt like it did when I placed one foot into the pool the first day of swim lessons. I wanted to run (and I think I may have done just that when I was a kid). Similar to childhood, anxiety took over me as I waded deeper and deeper into those unknown waters, and I made every excuse in the book. *I'm not ready for this. I don't want to almost drown again. This is not going to end well.*

At that party, I thought I knew how to swim or, at the very least, could teach myself as I went along. Nearly drowning and then having someone show me the correct way to swim proved me wrong. The same has gone with dating. After going through a disastrous relationship, I realized I don't know the correct way of doing things. I don't know what it looks or feels like to be in a healthy relationship. Dating in a healthy way feels foreign to me. Love far-fetched. And decent, godly, respectful men confusing to me.

And this is why I've had to go through a few trial and errors in dating to find out what should be normal and expected, and what I need in a relationship. Life has been full of lessons in this aspect the past few years. While I jumped headfirst into one relationship, the one this book has been about, there has been another relationship where I entered into it much slower than before.

Time for a shift in the story.

After my second date with the guy I talked about above (to my surprise, that attraction I felt was mutual), I fought a confusing mix of emotions. I liked him, and that scared me. I knew what the attraction and growing feelings I began to have for him meant, and in my mind, they meant nothing but trouble. I didn't want to step forward in this, yet at the same time, I very much did. So I cautiously crept forward in dating once more. However, things with him seemed different than what I've had in the past, and because everything felt different, I had a growing hope this was good and we had a chance of making a relationship work. But on the other hand, because of that excruciatingly slow reentrance into dating, I found myself with overwhelming anxiety and fears relearning how to date with a guarded heart while also fighting off small triggers that brought me back to old hurts.

Because we moved slowly in dating, the text that ended things and flashed across my screen after our second date stung, but it didn't break my heart. I cried that night, dried up my tears, and started the next day almost good as new. We decided to continue as friends, and I was totally okay with that. Or so we kept trying to tell ourselves. Logic kept warning me to set firm boundaries in our friendship, but the feelings for him that I was determined to ignore kept me responding to his daily conversation starters beginning the night after he broke things off. I began to psych myself up to have that hard conversation, but in reality, I was still holding onto a thread of hope that we would eventually give our relationship another chance. So I continued to brush off those warnings for a week. Just as I was ready to have that conversation with him due to feeling confused about our "friendship," he asked for a second chance. I felt peace in letting him take me on our third date, or our "second first date," and I continued to feel that peace and a growing happiness for a time as we decided to continue to date.

Time went by and continued to go by without any indication in where we were at in our relationship. There was no clarification on what we were, only that we were dating. We were basically boyfriend and girlfriend, but we never clarified and instead held to a no-label relationship. Even though we had agreed to take things slow, we were with each other more often than not. We progressed to a point that, if you had seen us out in public, you could tell we were a happy couple; however, we were not opening up emotionally. Sure, we were very comfortable with each other, and physical barriers were broken down as was normal, but anything deeper in our relationship was absent. I constantly felt confused as I never knew where I stood and was rapidly growing impatient in waiting for any clarity from him.

Week after week would go by and my unease would grow with each new day. Something wasn't right. I knew from past experience what justifying an unhealthy lifestyle and blatantly wrong actions would lead to, but that wasn't the problem here. I had known this man as a friend before we took it deeper, and I knew that he was a great guy. The problem was the absence of clarity and a state of confusion that left me with an unsettling feeling of being strung along.

I had to make a choice. I could continue to creep forward in this relationship and hope for a miracle of him fully committing to me but run the risk of drowning like I had in the past. Or, as much as I hated the thought, I could step out of those waters, chalk this one up to one more painful lesson, gain my bearings once more, and step back into that pool at a later time. The lessons I've learned kicked in, and I was able to swim back to safer waters before I completely lost my sense of direction. I knew what it felt like to drown and have a part of myself die, and as much as I wanted him, I desired more to never lose myself to unrequited love again. I knew what needed to come.

Goodbye Again

Here we go again.
I knew what it all meant. The unexplainable shifts in personality and effort, the beginnings of ghosting, the seemingly lack of care, and the undeniable feeling of emotional distance and physical barriers being introduced. It all led to one thing, and that thing was another broken heart. So I made the painful decision to step away. One year after the breakup that wrecked me, I went through another

painful breakup. That might not have been what you expected, huh? So many stories flood my TikTok feed too of how the right man came into the girl's life and swept her off her feet after her prior disastrous relationship. He helped put back a heart he didn't break… When she stopped looking, he came along…She thought she knew love before, but then he showed up…Yeah, I had hoped that might be my story with this man. But no, my story looked a bit more like a terrible reality TV show with a new guy breaking the female lead's heart each season.

This breakup, however, was different than the year prior. Why? I had to stay in contact with him.

Because of our schedules, I didn't see him for a while, and I had one month to get myself back together after our "second" breakup. That month was such a blessing because I knew that I couldn't handle seeing him again so soon after all that had happened between us. Not to mention that the pain of a failed relationship with him brought back so many reminders of the pain I had experienced a year prior. Let me tell you, that was a rough month. But it was also one of the best months.

I was once again dealing with the pain of missing someone who had quickly become one of my best friends and trying to recover the pieces of my heart that I had lost to him. Although not near as bad as my breakup with my other ex, the way our relationship ended still wounded me. I had to go through a time of processing all the emotions and hurt, and every new development regarding him post breakup would slice me once more. But while I was going through all of that, I found healing in a much better way than my little trial and errors the year before.

It was tempting to isolate myself and cry alone. I wanted to step away from our shared friend group because I didn't want to be reminded of him. The thought of seeing him again scared me because I didn't know what my reaction would be. I just didn't know if I would be able to handle it emotionally. However, I knew that, despite those fears, I feared the result of isolation even more. I remembered where that brought me before, and that terrified me more than anything. So I went against what I wanted to do and threw myself into the things that were difficult for me. Processing my thoughts, pain, and emotions with my close friends. Socializing and allowing myself to have fun. Pressing closer to God and still hanging out with the group of friends we shared instead of letting what happened between him and I destroy our friendships with the people to whom we had grown close.

During that month, I was able to get a good perspective on our breakup. I allowed myself to grieve, but I refused to stay stuck in that spot. I let others in on what I was feeling and accepted the words of truth they spoke into my life. Even though everything that was going on hurt like crazy, I had so much fun with my friends that month. I grew more in my faith. I learned more lessons of what I need and want in a relationship. And by the time that month came to an end and I was faced with seeing him for the first time post breakup, I could honestly say I was in a healthy place. Sure, I was still scared and I dreaded that meeting more than I can say. My heart did stop and panic momentarily froze me when I first spotted him, but recovery was swift. My mind did race with memories of spending afternoons in his arms and the many conversations we would have, and I did feel pain at the realization that there would never be an "us" again. There was no denying the tension and awkwardness between us; however, I remained confident in our decision to end our relationship and was able to stay in the same group of people as him without feeling an impending emotional breakdown. I was able to genuinely laugh and have fun, and with that, I found myself able to let him and our past go.

This doesn't mean there wasn't any pain involved in letting him go nor does it mean that there weren't difficult moments or hard days after seeing him again where it hurt a little more and the tears came with little prompting. It definitely was a process that took time. It does mean that I didn't let that pain control me. Through the grace of Jesus, I didn't let it keep me stuck in a rut. It didn't consume me this time. And even though it all hurt very badly, I was able to quickly see that a relationship together wasn't God's best for us, no matter how much I had wanted it. Saying goodbye to another man

I had cared for was undoubtedly difficult, but it definitely wasn't the end of my story that I know God is carefully writing.

Emotional Safeguards and Regret

"You have to tell him soon. I know it might feel weird to talk about, but he needs to know."

My best friend told these words to me as I was fighting anxiety over telling the man I had been dating about this book I'm writing. He knew that there was a book I was finishing up writing, but I had dodged any further conversation about it for almost two months. I wasn't ready to reach that level of vulnerability, and the guard I had put up around my heart was proving difficult to lower. But after getting to know him and becoming increasingly comfortable with him, I felt I was getting closer to spilling it all. Still the fears remained. *What if he's not going to care? What if he finds it weird that I'm writing a book about recovering from heartbreak while he and I are dating? He isn't opening up to me, so why should I be the first to open up my heart?*

Even with those fears swirling about in my mind, I knew it was time to begin the process of ripping away the Band-Aid I used to hide the scars marking my heart.

So I told him the general overview of this book, and he was supportive. And even though I didn't go into detail, it wasn't as hard as I thought it would be. It felt good to let him a little bit more into who I am. He didn't press for the whole story, and I felt immense relief that I could tell him on my own time as I learned to trust him more.

However, there came the momentary regret after we had broken up. *Why did I tell him about this? Why did I begin to be vulnerable and let him into who I am when it was all for nothing? He never tried to break those emotional barriers himself, so what was the point?* It seemed that all that left me with was another guy who knew a little too much about me now that we had to go our separate ways.

But here's the thing. I can focus on how it seemed pointless to open up just to get hurt again. I can rant about how the pain of losing someone close to you is not worth the vulnerability it takes to achieve that closeness. I can go on about how he didn't reciprocate and share anything deeper about himself and how it was all one-sided. Or I can focus on the positives. I can choose to see that, even though I had begun to let another guy who I don't have a future with see a side to me not many people saw, I *was* able to start to let him in. Remember that fear I had of not being able to open up and love again? I genuinely believed that the trauma and baggage from my past relationship would hinder me from ever doing that again, but this relationship proved me wrong. It was scary and hard, yes, but it was possible. And while he may know a little bit more about me than other people do, maybe it was also good for him. Maybe one day the guys I've been in relationships with can use what happened with us as lessons for the future like I have been able to do.

I don't regret our relationship. God used him in that place in my life for a season to continue to grow my faith in Jesus and highlight what standards I need to keep in the future. I no longer wish I can take back the things I shared with him because God might use that in his life just as He did in mine. I truly don't long to rewind the clock on either of my relationships because they proved to be seasons where my faith grew the most.

I also have to remind myself that even though I had started to be vulnerable with him, we didn't reach that point where he knew *everything* about me. I was still able to guard my heart and keep some emotional boundaries in place that allowed me to walk away without a destroyed heart. Severely bruised, yes, but not shattered. And thankfully, not hardened.

Soft Hearts Are Not Weak

Every move was excruciating. Even lying still, I continued to feel the searing pain shoot down my legs, all thanks to just my pride trying to keep up with my super fit parents when I decided to join them for a workout. It had been so long since I exercised that intensely, maybe since high school, and my muscles were screaming at me to never put myself through that torture again. My body was no longer used to working like that anymore, and for the next few days, walking was nearly impossible. After spending a day resting my legs as much as I could, I eventually had to start moving once more, slowly adding back in more things to my daily life as the pain and soreness wore off. As pathetic as this sounds, I felt like I had to learn to walk again.

Isn't it the same with dating, relationships, and love? We get burned and jumping back into the game feels as impossible as walking after a killer workout. Eventually, though, the soreness begins to fade and what once seemed unlikely to ever happen again becomes a reality. Muscle begins to replace what was atrophied. The wound gradually starts to close. Scars form, yet they are just a testament to a story that has shaped you. Not meant to harden your heart, they are guarding it and providing you with necessary caution and forming future decisions to protect it. They are the protective fencing around what should remain a soft heart. Access to that heart is hard-won but still very much possible.

What is a soft heart? A soft heart is one that still feels deeply. That dreams big no matter the odds and takes hope in the possibility of those dreams one day coming to fruition. It is a heart that still loves completely and passionately because of the softening from the complete and passionate love it receives from Jesus. It is one that still cries at the injustice of a messed-up world and continues to feel the pain that cuts and bruises invoke. It aches with the pressures of unfulfilled desires and feels the strain of every external push and pull. Yet the soft heart doesn't allow the bitterness from the seemingly daily hurts and wounds to infiltrate and sink its roots deep within. It sees the overheard darkness and acknowledges the impending gloom but chooses to see beyond the dense clouds to the rays of glorious light from the Son piercing the black of night. The soft heart chooses to continue on with hope when the world screams at it to give up. It rises up against the tide instead of allowing itself to be pulled down *deep, deep, deep* into the dismal waves. This soft heart pushes back against the fear nipping at all sides to move forward in love after love was what seemed to have crushed it in the first place. It chooses to stand tall against the tower of mounting doubts and seemingly endless questions and then plunges forward into living in fearless abandon, giving itself wholly over to the love of Jesus.

I don't know about you, but sometimes I feel like a soft heart is just an invitation to be trampled on. I think of letting myself fall in love once more and my stomach churns with dread. I've caught myself on more than one occasion scoffing at the thought of a future with my heart in the hands of someone else. *Never again.* The imagination of empowering someone new with the keys to my heart only for me to be left utterly defenseless and powerless instills a hand-shaking, mind-numbing anxiety and deep-rooted fear. *I won't survive if I have to go through this again*, I've told myself. Layers of hurts have embedded in the walls of my heart, and the temptation to allow them to remain as an impenetrable, protective covering can sometimes be irresistible. It would be so easy to allow the hardness and bitterness to take over and consume me, to keep me in a seemingly safe haven away from all potentials of hurts and traumas, to distance myself with a bulletproof glass around my heart. But here's the thing.

Hard hearts shatter easily.

When you have a lump of clay and you mold it into a vase, after you finish and let it dry, it hardens. The forming is done and the result seems great. It was easy to let the clay dry out. But what happens when you take that vase and toss it onto the hardwood floor? It shatters. Into a million pieces. Shards flying every which direction and hiding themselves under furniture and rugs only to be found months later after being pierced from stepping onto one of the sharp remnants. The cleanup is tedious and time-consuming, and you are never guaranteed a whole vase after gluing the pieces back together. The jagged edges form visible scars up and down the patched-up vase. The glue adds yet another layer of hardness. The vase is knocked down again. And then the process starts once more.

But imagine the lump of clay never hardening. Imagine water continuously being sprayed onto it to keep it soft. If you take that softened vase and throw it down, it will be disfigured. Bent and misshapen but not beyond repair. Even if the clay somehow splits in half, it's much easier to put the pieces together than it is when it's hardened. The Potter takes the clay and pushes out the bent areas and smooths out the sharp lines caused by the impressions left behind by the outside world. And before you know it, the soft clay is back to where it was before. Or maybe it is shaped into a new, beautiful creation. The work to keep it soft is hard, yes, but it remains pliable and bounces back faster from being knocked down and pushed around. The shaping back into place is painful, but imagine how much more so when the sharp, jagged edges of a hardened vase are poking and prodding each other, serving as constant reminders of the brokenness.

No matter how many times a soft lump of clay, or a soft heart, is broken, it can be molded back into shape. It is still painful but much less so than a hardened, bitter heart being pieced back together.

Maybe soft hearts are worth it after all.

Our society can place such emphasis on being strong, independent, and self-sufficient when it comes to our hearts. We get broken, and the toxic message our wounded selves receive is, "This is why you shouldn't open yourself up. You're better off alone." Hardened hearts are perceived as a sign of strength. An indicator that you can stand up for yourself and not let life knock you down again and again. But in reality, a hardened heart is just one that has been poisoned by the fatal waters of bitterness. A heart that is at risk for repeated breaking. One that crumbles at every nudge but keeps a mask of serenity plastered on the outside.

On the contrary, soft hearts may seem weak to the outside world, but they are anything but weak. It takes strength to get up every morning and choose to not let the bitterness overtake the heart and bleed through every action and spoken word. The soft heart fights for transparency to be a trademark of its life and allows the tears to fall when needed. It draws on courage from Jesus to open itself up to love again. It sees the risk of being hurt once more yet laughs in the face of fear because it knows that even if it gets broken again, its Maker will mold it back together. Soft hearts look for the beauty among the ashes and choose joy even when everything around tries to pull it into a dark, ugly pit of depression. It takes courage to put an end to the choke-hold the past has and instead step into the freedom of new beginnings. A soft heart remains pliable and easily molded by its Maker when shifting seasons try its strength and durability. Soft hearts are not weak.

Shifting Seasons

Just as the beautiful, refreshing hope of spring turned into the scorching heat of summer, so the change in her heart and soul took place. The season of a bright, blooming love turned into being repeatedly burned and left painful marks. Gone was the cherished love that infiltrated her heart as she inadvertently plunged into the coming darkness, resembling the summer turning into fall and not unlike the clocks rewinding to provide lingering blackness and earlier twilights. As the leaves shriveled up and died, cold and forlorn on the frozen ground, so did parts of her heart. The winter in her soul was comparable in misery and blindness to a harrowing blizzard with drifts of snow trapping one inside a deserted house with a fire barely large enough to keep one alive. It was frigid and dark, and the chill permeated so deep within her she feared she would never be warm again.

But it wouldn't stay this way forever.

In the same manner that the earthly seasons shift, the seasons of her life began to change. The snow melted to reveal small, tender shoots of new plants, tentative hope beginning to take root once more in her thawing heart. The sun began to shine a little clearer and slightly longer with each passing day, and the deadened, frozen areas chipped away to reveal themselves as stronger and more resilient. The dormant days spent in the cold rejuvenated the spirit within her and prepared the soil of her heart for the days to come.

Maybe the time spent in the winter actually reflected the Son off the blinding white snow banks accumulated around her heart. It could be that the dismal fall purged her life of anything that was toxic. The intense summer days possibly were refining with fire the areas of her heart that she couldn't change on her own. Perhaps the giddy springtime was a reminder to cling only to the purest form of love and simultaneously hope for a replica of that on earth, imperfect though it may be.

In this, she discovered the purpose for the shifting seasons, and she found that, in their own unique way, each season was infinitely beautiful and something to be deeply treasured.

Thwarted Stories

It wasn't supposed to be like this. When I was younger, I had imagined my life to look very differently at twenty-four. Married, settled down in a house in the country with a big wraparound porch on some land with a couple of kids running around. I didn't picture twenty-four looking like spending another Saturday night alone with a glass of wine and a half-eaten box of Crumbl cookies on my kitchen counter.

As a child, my mind spun up a story of meeting the love of my life at a young age and walking down the aisle in early adulthood. So you can imagine me thinking eighteen would be different than what it was. I was saying goodbye to my grandmother at eighteen instead of reserving her a seat up front at my wedding. And life didn't pan out like I wanted it to when my early twenties came and went with my dreams of marriage and children remaining unfulfilled with each passing year. Instead, I was stuck struggling with feeling as if I was married to my highly stressful job and the drama and headaches that came along with it. When I finally thought those dreams of mine were going to come true, my midtwenties started on rocky footing as life threw me for a loop when I broke up with the man I had loved. And there is no telling what the rest of my twenties will look like.

This wasn't how my life was supposed to play out.

I think my love for writing can backfire in that I have all of these plots and storylines in my head just waiting to be put to paper. I have these ideas for stories that I think will be great, and then that desire to write a plot carries over into my own reality. When what I think may be an amazing chapter in the story of my life doesn't play out like I wanted it to, I have to remind myself that I'm not the author of that book. I don't know what the end of the story looks like for me. I have no clue what the next chapter will hold. For goodness sake, there is no telling what the next sentence will be. And my writer's heart and, if we're being honest, the humanly desire for control make me balk at that thought.

This is where surrender comes into play. It's hard to have a kneeling posture with hands wide open, giving all we have to the Father, when all we want to do is stand on our tiptoes and hold tightly to anything we can grasp to have some semblance of control in our lives. So we can have some clue as to what is going to happen, we play and replay possible scenarios in our minds to prepare ourselves for what may come. If we can cling onto some piece of control, we feel like we have somewhat of an anchor in the midst of the waves pushing us back and forth. In the unknown of this craziness we call life, it's hard to release the need for control. It's so very hard. And, my friend, I know it's just flat-out scary. I understand.

But here's the hard-to-swallow truth of it all. We can't control what we never had control of in the first place. We may trick ourselves into thinking we have some semblance of control in the way our lives play out. We have free will, absolutely, but not one thing or one event, not one hurt or one joy, *nothing* happens outside of God's control.

I know that's a hard truth to accept when life throws one too many punches and you've been knocked down and pushed around too many times to count. Our human brains can't comprehend how God can be in total control yet allow trauma in our lives. There really isn't a sufficient answer to satisfy the desire to know the reasons behind the heartbreak.

But I do know this. Through all of the chaotic and painful changes in our lives, through the days that cause us to drag our feet and hang our heads in defeat, through the soul-sucking heartaches and depression, there is One who never changes. He stays constant throughout the menacing waves that rock our lives. Jesus walks on water and lovingly holds His hand out if only we would grab hold of it. And once we cling to Him, we're safe. The waves might not calm until He gives the command, but we no longer are being pulled into the depths of the sea. We no more need to focus on the dismal gray of our surroundings that seem to never change. Instead, we can hold in view the glorious light of the Son piercing the black of night. Once our perspective changes from a victim mindset to having victory through the One who has already been proclaimed Victor, hope begins to infiltrate those once-dark spaces of the heart. When the storms of life come, and *they will come* because we are not promised an easy life, we have a mainstay that steadies us and keeps our heads above water. We can begin to trust that our story is not over nor has it ever been thwarted. We are exactly in the chapter of our lives where we need to be, and God will use it for His glory and our good.

Empty Arms but Full Heart

Whatever season you're walking through, remember that there is always beauty to be found in it. If you're single, I know how hard it is. I feel your pain. I experience those days when it seems like finding love is all I can think about. The moments hit often when all you want is someone to talk to about what you never tell anyone else and to share the burdens of life with a partner. There always seems to be a longing to fall into the arms of the person you love, to have a shoulder to cry on and a beautiful soul to laugh with. I know so well the desire to love and be loved and to have unfulfilled dreams of a husband and children. The tears haunt me too when I go home alone to an empty house. I get it; it's extremely hard.

But it can also be beautiful.

I know I probably won't get this time as a single woman back again. One day, there might be a husband and children to take care of, but for now, it's just me. While there can definitely be a depressing perspective to that, there's an encouraging, hopeful perspective to which we should shift our minds.

In this time of my life, I don't have the added worries of caring for a family. There's no extra laundry to fold or dishes to wash. I don't have to be woken up multiple times through the night when a child can't sleep or plan my schedule around my husband and children. Don't get me wrong; I would love to have all of that and I know it is absolutely worth the sleepless nights and stress, but without them, I have more opportunities to do things I wouldn't be able to do while married. I have the ability to stay out late with my small groups studying the Bible and socializing. There's no need to check in with a husband about where I'm going or have to decline lending a hand to someone in the middle of a move because I have children to think about. This time is the chance to join all the social events I want, build lasting friendships and go on spontaneous vacations with my friends.

Without this time, it would've been way less likely that I would've written this book. All of this stemmed from countless late nights and hours upon hours spent in coffee shops on the weekends. It was difficult enough to juggle this with working two jobs, my family and social life, and just basic life stuff (all of those months of insomnia prepared me for this). I can't imagine how much of a slower process this would've been if I had a boyfriend or husband during this whole time of writing. Honestly though, through no fault of his, having a man in my life those couple of months did slow this down some. So I guess I can picture where I would be at now with this writing process if I was in a relationship the entire time.

Remember that solo trip that I had wanted to take to run from the pain? Well, I finally did go on a beach getaway by myself so many months later, and the timing was perfect. On the coldest weekend of the year when all of us confused Floridians had to figure out how much to let the faucets drip to prevent the pipes from freezing, I was bundled up in my aunt and uncle's beach house typing away on my laptop and praying over this book. This solo trip helped me not only focus on writing but to also gain a new perspective on all the changes going on in my life. And then I did it again six months later. The stillness and quiet that marked these vacations is already hard to come by, but once a family enters the picture, it will become a rarity.

While I can put a positive spin on that left ring finger being bare and that last name being unchanged, there's still that undeniable longing for something more. And that's okay. God made each of us with these beautiful dreams and desires, but just because we have these desires and dreams doesn't mean we put our lives on hold until they come to fruition. It means we learn to thrive in where we are and look for the good in each season we're given.

Using the season you are in (but really don't want to be in, if we're being honest) does not mean you need to do something drastic with your life to make the time meaningful. While one person may be called to write a book or another called to an overseas mission trip, someone may be called to take a step of faith to just join a church or begin to serve. It may look like spending more time in the Bible instead of social media or it may mean choosing to invest more of yourself in a friendship. Making the most of the time given isn't doing something great in the world's eyes but being faithful to where God is calling us and stepping out in faith and obedience in what He wants us to do.

And that is how we have full hearts and full lives despite having empty arms and empty houses.

The Glow-Up

Here comes the section that everybody wants to learn about. How do we make an ex jealous and full of regret that he let a good thing go? Are you ready for this piece of info? Because I'm about to share the holy grail to this.

You don't.

I'm sorry, what?

That's right. We don't. We don't try to make an ex regret letting us go and keep him coming back. That's not what life is about. Begin to work on yourself without the intention of your ex seeing you in person or on Instagram living your best life without him. I've tried the whole "make him jealous" glow-up, and it only left me worn out, unsatisfied, and empty. Work on yourself so you can live your best life. Period. No strings attached.

Let. Him. Go.

After a breakup, it's common that one or both of the people in the relationship experience what is commonly known as a *glow-up*. I'm all for a glow-up if done with the correct motives. And not just the physical kind of glow-up. The best kind you can have is one that starts from within. These are changes that should be made no matter what stage of life you're in.

Now that we've gotten that ex out of the way, let's just jump right into ways to glow-up, shall we?

Prioritize quiet time. The best thing anyone can do, whether post breakup or not, is to prioritize quiet time with Jesus. Self-isolation is my go-to coping mechanism, and it had become as self-isolating as you can imagine. So much so that my quiet time with Jesus was almost nonexistent. It was terrible. It seemed there was no end to the pain and fears as my days were never focused on spending time with my Savior.

Carve out a time to spend every day in prayer and in Bible study. Keep to that time each day, and it will soon become a habit that you can't live without. Mornings are the best time to do this so as to start the day off on the right foot, and for me, if I don't do it first thing in the morning, it becomes less likely that I will do it at any other point in the day. Through the work day, if you can, listen to worship music or podcasts to help fill your heart with and help you dwell on the things of Christ (Phil. 4:8). I've also found that spending some time in the Word as the last thing I do at night helps to refocus my mind on the goodness of God and provides peace when life is overwhelming and sleep feels impossible.

When I finally got my priorities straight and began to actually put Jesus first and foremost, my life radically changed. Starting my day off on the right foot with Bible study and prayer time in the mornings, ending it with the same, and filling my day with things that pointed me to Jesus changed my mindset. It shifted the weight I was carrying to the capable arms of my Savior. It wasn't perfect and it will never be perfect this side of eternity, but it was the best decision I could ever make.

It takes so much discipline, and there will definitely be days when you don't feel like spending time in the Word and in prayer, but it fills your soul with what is meant to be in there. We were created to worship the King of kings, and there is no better way to do that than to let Him reside in every part of our hearts and every part of our lives.

Join a small group. Words cannot explain how impactful this was for me. I had been involved with some Bible studies and small groups over the years, but since entering my twenties, I was unable to find a group I could click with. And honestly, I didn't try too hard to find one. For a time, I had joined an online women's Bible study, and we met over Zoom. Although everyone was very sweet and welcoming, there was still something missing for me. The ladies in this group were much older and in different life stages than me, so it was difficult for me to connect with any of them. There also wasn't much accountability with a Zoom Bible study, so there were many weeks when I skipped.

A couple of months after my breakup, I found myself becoming increasingly reclusive. The only times I would leave my house was to go grocery shopping or if it was to spend time with family. I made excuses for everything else. Each outing was a small victory to me and more tiring than I can describe. As this started to get worse and the depression I was struggling with became more noticeable, I knew I was at the point where I had to make myself get out of my house and do something that did not involve necessity or family.

During a very rare time of confidence and conviction (this was nothing but a God-thing), I began to search for local Bible studies and came across one that was connected with the church my brother and cousin attend and that was geared toward women my age. After calling my cousin for info, one thing led to another and two days later I was walking up to a stranger's house to attend a small group with people I had never met. I was so nervous that I almost walked back to my car to go home. I felt like, because it was hard to summon up the energy to socialize and paste on a fake smile to be polite, these ladies would think I was rude. But these women welcomed me with open arms and made me feel so comfortable right off the bat. Within just a few minutes, I had relaxed, socialized without effort, and was able to smile without pretense. Immediately, I knew that this group was a group that loved Jesus immensely because of the love they showed every stranger that walked through that door.

To be plugged in with a small group is so empowering. It might not be easy to find a group, but they are out there and it is worth the search. It's scary to step out into the unknown with people you don't know, but when Jesus is at the center, it's beautiful and life-giving. I'm now involved with two small groups, and the people in both groups quickly became the people I run to for advice and wisdom. These are friendships I value, and our times together are days I look forward to the most.

Get involved with a church. Before my breakup, I wasn't attending church services regularly. I would join my family for Bible studies they would have where we would sometimes be joined by family friends, but I was missing a key component to my spiritual walk. I made the excuse that I live in a smaller town with not many church options, but let's face it. I live in the South; there's a church on every street corner. That was just a pathetic excuse. There were issues with some churches that I knew of and considered joining, but I didn't take the time and effort to actually search for a home church. Truthfully, I was judgmental of and closed off to churches I did not grow up in. It wasn't until after I joined the small group that I decided to give the church that the group was connected with a chance.

I went into it hesitant. I didn't want to get involved with a church that may later on down the road split up because I have dealt with that kind of drama before. Social anxiety also kept me from jumping into it with much enthusiasm, and this is a church that has hundreds of people in each service. Thankfully, my cousin and brother already attended, so at least I wouldn't have to go in alone.

After that first service I went to, I felt I had found a church I could attend and grow with spiritually. Before I knew it, I had joined other groups through the church and found myself in a community who inspired me to work on my relationship with Jesus like never before.

Being surrounded by godly community is priceless and something we can so easily take for granted. Take the opportunity now to build strong friendships and to find a group of believers who become your prayer warriors and you theirs. Make spending time worshipping Jesus with others a priority instead of an option. We were made for fellowship with the body of Christ.

Serve. Perspective is everything, and perspective can easily be warped when we are going through a rough patch in our lives. We can become so laser-focused on our own problems that we fail to see that people around us are living with struggles as well. This makes serving vital.

When we begin to shift our line of vision from ourselves to others, we start to see that we all have our own difficulties. And when we move toward others by serving, we can find joy and even some level of healing of our own pain.

Serving in my church in the children's program is a balm for my heart. To be a small part of being a light in these children's lives and to give their parents a chance to worship and listen to the sermon without interruption brings me joy. How much better to spend our free time putting somebody needs before our own instead of sitting in our own frustrations and pain?

Serving looks different for everyone as we all have our own strengths. Whether that is serving coffee or volunteering in the children's program at church to lending a hand to someone who needs help with a home project or bringing a meal to a sick family or new parents, there is always a way we can care for others. Look for ways to serve in your church, your community, and anywhere you are placed in life.

Set and work toward goals. This may sound cliché, but right now, in whatever kind of season of waiting you are in, is the time to devote to your goals. There will still be goals you will want to achieve in every stage of life, but think about the ones that you can really throw yourself into now that may be more difficult to focus on in another life stage.

For me, I started to live as if I might never get married. Yes, I still hope for it, pray for it, and believe it will happen, but I'm not going to place my life on hold until that day comes. So instead of waiting for Prince Charming to come riding into my life and provide me my dream home, I'm working toward doing that myself. I'm saving for a down payment and preparing for the day when I can begin to make my own home. I'm working on paying off any debt and hopefully creating habits that keep me out of debt. Finishing this book is on the top of my list of goals as is continuing to write more books. I recently learned that my supervisors at my job want to see me move up in our company, so advancing my career has also become one of my aspirations.

What are your goals? What are you hoping to achieve in this time you're given? We may not be able to reach everything that we are hoping for, but it is so much better to go for it instead of sitting around and waiting for something that may or may not happen.

Work toward becoming the healthiest version of yourself. Spiritually. Emotionally. Physically. Quiet time with Jesus and building godly community fall into the spiritual category. Emotionally, work through past traumas and baggage. If you think a counselor would be of benefit, book those sessions. Take this time to sort through any hang-ups you may have.

And here comes the part everyone thinks of when a glow-up is mentioned. Become the healthiest version of yourself physically as well. Not to make an ex jealous and full of regret like I had hoped would happen at one point, but because your body is the temple of God, and we should treat our bodies with care and respect.

Because I do hope and pray to be married and have children one day, now is the time to get my body into shape. I've been using this time to gain back the weight I had lost and become fit. I want to be able to still get around easily when I'm older, so I need to put in the work now.

Working on improving our physical appearance is not wrong. It is healthy and godly because our bodies are the temple of God, and we are called to take care of them. Where it begins to get messy is when we put our confidence in our appearance and our sole focus on physical self-improvement. Our confidence should be so rooted in Jesus and our identity so secure in Him, that our beauty shines from within. Our outward appearance should only be a highlight to that.

Have fun. I don't think any of us want to be eighty years old and looking back on our younger years with regret. I don't want to tell my children someday of the times when I was single, and it sound something like this. *Well, let me try to remember what I did when I was single…I sat in my living room most nights, eating ice cream and watching rom-coms, crying. Yep, that's about it. Oh, and I worked over forty hours a week, so there's that!*

Absolutely not. Let's rewrite the script.

I enjoyed time with the people in my life. Most of my days were spent going on spontaneous beach day trips, movie nights with family, pool days and playing sports with friends, small group dinners and sleepovers with my girlfriends even though we were adults. I took solo trips and went to so many conferences and retreats. I had so. Much. Fun.

I'm not saying that it's always going to be easy and that it's always going to be full of happy laughter and genuine smiles. Some days will suck. Sometimes, the loneliness hits a little harder. There will still be times when having fun seems difficult and the pain makes itself known. This is normal. There have been times when I've had a full day of being with people I love and making so many memories, but as soon as I'm alone, the floodgates open and the tears fall. This, however, is not the rule. It doesn't make you ungrateful or discontent to desire someone special to share your life with while at the same time thriving in life. Just don't stay stuck in that rut.

Keep pushing through. Find things, activities, and people that promote your love for God and bring a smile to your face. Meet new people. Learn something you've always wanted to learn. Do what seems fun to you. Life doesn't have to be put on hold until your relationship status changes. Live life *despite* your relationship status.

Contentment Is Not the Goal

The right one will come when you're not looking.

When you learn to be content, that's when the Lord knows you're ready for a spouse.

Insert dramatic eye roll here.

Well-intended statements don't always come across as helpful and encouraging. And if you're single like me, they can make you go from being single to…Well, *painfully* single. Sometimes, I feel like it's better not to say anything and just let things be because I've heard those statements *for years,* and they are *not* helpful. And honestly, it's made me feel as if I'm not doing something correctly. Like I haven't reached this elite status of godliness that God deems is the right level to give a spouse and I have this particular art I need to master before being allowed to level up. It's as if everybody else has reached the next stage and I'm lagging behind because of who knows what. It's like tattooing "Failure" on my forehead in bold letters.

We treat contentment as a status to attain. A skill to be flawlessly executed when tested. A permanent shift from desiring something to being happy-go-lucky and forgetting that those desires even existed. We strive for unattainable perfectionism over gracious progress.

The letter to the church of Philippians is widely known for its overarching theme of joy and contentment. When Paul wrote this letter, he was in dire circumstances. He was chained to a guard in prison. *In prison.* Arrested for spreading the good news of salvation through Jesus Christ, his patience, endurance, and joy were tested severely. I think we tend to think of Paul as this guy chained to the Roman guard who was deliriously oblivious to his surroundings. We might go so far as to think he was laughing it up with his cellmates and just pretending like he was on a beach sipping a piña colada to forget the reality of the dark, cold prison cell in which he was being held. Always singing. Always smiling. Always happy. Never down about the situation. Never questioning the circumstances. Always *joyful* and most definitely, constantly *content.* Like Paul had reached the much-coveted elite status of contentment and surrender to the Lord and didn't even bat an eye when life was hard because he just no longer desired to be out of prison.

I don't believe this is true.

While I do know that Paul handled persecution and imprisonment far better than many of us in the twenty-first century could have if we were faced with what he went through, I also know that he was just as human as the rest of us. He wasn't telling his readers that he had attained that desirable position of joyfulness and contentment as in a completed work but that he was *choosing* joy and contentment. The goal wasn't to be free of internal struggles or free from the desire for circumstances to change. Rather, the goal was to continue to *choose* thankfulness when the temptation to grumble and complain crept in. To *choose* to sing praises to the sovereign Lord instead of letting despair be a lord over our souls. To *choose* to believe, even in the midst of the messy, heartbreaking times that leave us questioning everything, that God is in control and His grace is sufficient. To *choose* to trust that God is bigger than our circumstances, doubts, and wants. To *choose* surrender of our lives, dreams, desires, and plans to the Author of our stories.

Contentment is not the goal. Contentment is a choice.

We are still going to stumble about in this quest to choose contentment every day. It's not something that we wake up and choose and then never have an issue with again. It's a day-by-day, moment-by-moment choice to look for the good and find something to be joyful about. Even in the most dire and painful of times, we always have something for which we can be grateful.

Contentment isn't about not having desires or wishing for something different. It's what we do with those desires and how we let it affect our lives. There will be times when you feel like you are satisfied with where God has you in life, but then the next day, or maybe even the next minute, you're struggling with trusting if He knows what is actually best for you. Those thoughts and feelings of discontent are natural, but what we do with those feelings is what matters. As long as we are on this earth, we will fight the temptations to give into despair over our circumstances.

Instead of waiting for the next chapter of your life to start or waiting for your desires to shift or for that "feeling" of contentment to kick in, start living life now. Choose to let go of the need to know what happens next or when things will change. Place those unknowns into the more-than-capable hands of Jesus and choose to surrender each moment to Him even when it's hard.

That is contentment.

Handing Over the Keys

The heart is a fragile thing. It's the easiest to break and the hardest to heal. In the blink of an eye, it can be shattered into a million pieces. Each shard has to be picked up and painstakingly reassembled.

The process of piecing together that heart is slow and excruciating. It involves weeping on the bathroom floor, countless sleepless nights, and headaches that always seem to linger. Denial of the situation and hope that the one who broke that heart would come back and make everything right are constant companions for the first little while.

Eventually, though, anger creeps in and the battered heart begins to perceive what it couldn't when it thought it was loved. The blinders are lifted and, through the new lens of pain and betrayal, it sees the deceit and manipulation that marked the relationship. The facade that caused it to fall into deep, oblivious love fades away to reveal the accurate character of the one who crushed the heart and even the character of the crushed heart itself.

Profound fear of future rejection and repeated mistakes come into play as scars form and walls around the heart are unintentionally built. There's a strong desire to close off oneself from ever tumbling into unrequited adoration again, to never have to experience the wounds caused by the sharp knife of deception once more, and to avoid further smashing the hopes and dreams of a helpless romantic.

But then, just as the heart begins to assume it won't recover, a shift in perspective happens. Light begins to trickle into the dark recesses of the heart and takes root. The days don't seem as long and the nights aren't as lonely as tentative hope makes an appearance.

Dawning on the increasingly confident heart is the truth that it finally starts to accept: it was never alone and has always been loved. No amount of pain could pry it from the hands of the One by whom it was formed. He is constantly present to catch each anguished tear and hear every broken prayer. Gently guiding the way through this dark season, He uses the time to teach the most invaluable lessons and refines the heart to closer resemble what He intended it to be.

Much to the surprise of the comforted heart, the ability to truly forgive presents itself and provides freedom and immense peace despite the lack of closure. The strength for that forgiveness, the heart understands, only comes from the grace and absolution it received from Jesus.

Even though rough days are still to be had, the heart slowly starts to move on and let go of what was and what could've been. It finds its confidence in Christ alone and is eager to see what the future may hold. It looks back and counts numerous blessings, allowing the lessons provided to reform it and holding fast to God-given promises. While there is no timeline for healing and growth, the heart takes courage that beauty will come from the ashes and begins to find joy once more because the heart is guarded by its Savior.

What Shouldn't Have Been Should've Been

As the days crept by and time inched closer to the one-year anniversaries of us meeting online, meeting in person, and becoming official, I wrestled with the seeming cruelty of it all. He should've been here. We should've been reminiscing together on those days and be in amazement together on just how fast time flies. He should've been with me to celebrate me turning twenty-four. Family vacations he had promised to join. Those hard days of work stress and feeling overwhelmed when I just needed his support. The simple, carefree days when all we would've done is slow-dance in the kitchen and share our dreams. I should've been there to welcome him home from the work trips he had. His family events for which he was supposedly eager to bring me to his hometown. I should've still been a phone call away for the difficult nights that kept him from falling asleep.

We should've been only two hours away from each other instead of a lifetime apart.

He chose not to be here, and that's okay. I chose to stop fighting for a relationship that wasn't meant to be, and I'm okay. God has a much better plan, and I can now see the good in it all. With that, I know he *shouldn't* be here with me.

What I had thought should've been was only a fantasy. The pain and heartbreak were cruel, but what wasn't cruel at all was that God, in His infinite love and wisdom, had something different in mind for me. While part of me can still ache from the scars left behind, I'm now at a much better place in life where I *know* we were not made for each other. I can look back with some fondness to those few good days where we were carefree and our future together seemed plausible and likely, yet not become caught up in longing for that time to return. Those long days when my heart would be broken by thoughtless words, careless actions, and traitorous leaving no longer have their claws sinking deep within me. Although the scars left are uncomfortable when stretched, they no longer drag me through bouts of intense pain and I no longer helplessly let it pull me along. Through the grace of God, I've learned to allow the past to reshape me for the better.

And life looks so much more beautiful now. Not beautiful in a way that everything is perfect and I don't have difficult days but beautiful in a way that I can clearly see God working in my life. So many good things have sprung up from that dark season of my life that make me pause in wonder of how good of a God we serve. I can't imagine my life without all the many blessings that have come from experiencing that broken heart, and I truly don't regret any of it because of the personal growth it brought into my life.

Growth isn't the absence of hard days or unruly emotions. It's not the sudden disappearance of memories, both good and bad. It isn't our circumstances changing to magically reveal a new person on the other side but what we choose to do throughout those circumstances that will eventually lead to a changed person.

What I've come to realize over time is that while he was not good to me or good for me relationship-wise, he *was* good for my growth. Just not in the way that would result in a lasting relationship with him. And while our relationship itself may not have reflected Christ, what *did* reflect Him was the priceless lessons and beauty He brought from the pain. What *did* reflect Him was the overwhelming love and support from those He placed in my life. The strengthened faith that came as a result *did* reflect Him.

The times my heart was broken and the nights I spent crying myself to sleep eventually eased away. The fears that swirled in me began to be replaced by irrefutable truths. Joy became easier to find in Jesus, and my identity became unshakeable in Him. And when those days of heartbreak and nights full of tears ended up repeating themselves a year later, I knew where to run and I knew how to cope. Because of the past, I knew without a shadow of a doubt that Jesus is the only way to get through the difficulties, and because my identity was finally rooted in Him, healing was a bit easier and I had more hope. During the times of seemingly unending pain and one failed relationship after another, God was working for my good, and even though I couldn't see it in the moment, growth was happening.

And now I can confidently say, because I can trust in God's intricate, perfect, and incomparable plan for my life, "This is what should've been."

You Are Not Too Much

While there have been so many lessons throughout this time of breaking up and healing and then breaking up and healing once more, the one that has stood out the most is learning to know my worth.

We tend to underestimate how invested we become in the people we date, especially when the relationship becomes serious. We overlook the effects this person has on us, and sometimes, we become dependent on them and who they say we are. Our lives become so intertwined together that it's hard to remember who you were without them and how to live with their absence if that time were to ever come. Sometimes, we settle in their treatment of us and refuse to believe we can do better. With a devalued perspective of ourselves, we accept devaluing treatment from others and begin to believe that we are just too much. This is a twisted truth.

Here's the reality. You will be too much. *For the wrong person.*

The wrong person will look at you and want to be with you. They will like what they see and may even love you in their own way. However, they love the surface-level you. The uncomplicated, superficial you that is present at the beginning of dating. But when you start to reveal the layers of your heart, it becomes too much for them. They see the depth of your emotions, and it scares them to no end. As they learn of your boundaries and standards, they are unable to rise up to meet them for any number of reasons. Immaturity, commitment issues, or fear just to name a few. The wrong person then starts to make you feel unworthy of love. You begin to feel like you are asking for too much from them or you are just too much as a person. The wrong person will promote the lie that you need to change something about who you are in order for them to be able to love you and stay with you. The wrong person will love the "easy" version of you but run at the slightest sign of difficulty.

This, what this person makes you feel and the lack of value they ascribe to you, *is not who you are.*

Who you are in Jesus is a beautiful and complete child of God. He declares over you that you are fearfully and wonderfully made. He loves you regardless of what you've done with no strings attached. He welcomes you with open arms no matter what. Without any shame, He claims you as His. You are worthy because He made you worthy. You have infinite value because you are His creation. Beautifully pursued, wholly accepted, and dearly loved.

He knows what you need and who you need, and if He has marriage in store for you one day, then He has created the *right person* for you.

The right person will look at you and want to be with you. That's how it starts. They will see the surface level you that intrigues them and will want to dive in deeper. They will tear down every carefully placed wall around your heart and fall in love with each layer of you even when it seems complicated. The right person will encourage you to express your emotions no matter how messy they can get.

They won't laugh or walk away when faced with your vulnerability and tears; instead, they will hold you and cry with you, listening to you share the depths of your soul or working to fix a wrong if needed. In return, they will open up their heart to be seen and known by you. They will consistently remind you not only of your physical beauty but, more importantly, your inner beauty and your immeasurable value. They will know they don't deserve to have you but will work to keep you anyways. The right person will speak truth into you and point you to Jesus. They won't leave you confused and lonely but will bring clarity and will always seek to be close to you. They won't leave you waiting or make promises they can't keep, and they will stick by your side through thick and thin. The right person will love every single version of you, and that love will only grow in times of difficulty.

The right person will definitely not be perfect, but they will be perfect for you. And because love is a two-way street, while you are praying for that right person to come along, become that right person for them.

Love Never Fails

Love is patient. It isn't the absence of complications; it's the determination to work through the hard times and arguments to come to a resolution. It is bearing with each other through the attitudes and emotional breakdowns. Love remains a steadfast anchor through the highs and lows.

Love is kind. It speaks gently and selflessly. It's the random flowers picked from the side of the road and the thought-out candlelit dinners. But it's also the midnight conversations when one can't sleep. The tender care when sickness hits and the rescheduling of life to be present for each other in the difficult moments. It's surprising the other with a clean house and a prepared meal to come home to when they have a hard day at work. Love is the voice of reason and encouragement when the outside voices scream the opposite.

Love does not boast. Love isn't picture-perfect and Instagram-worthy; it's an imperfect picture that reflects a perfect love from

Jesus. It doesn't pretend to the world that life is smooth sailing nor does it hide behind rose-colored glasses. It lets outside help in to shed light and impart wisdom. Love seeks out the advice from others in order to be the best they can be for the person they love. Love also doesn't take pride in making one jealous nor does it flaunt its own good deeds.

Love is not proud. It accepts its own flaws and the flaws of the other person. It works to better itself and humbly accepts correction when needed. It seeks to know how to better love the other and what needs to change in order to make a life together work. Love knows how to apologize when wrong, extend forgiveness when wronged, and accept forgiveness for themselves.

Love does not dishonor others. It doesn't talk negatively about the other behind their back. It doesn't pit people against each other for the sake of winning an argument. It speaks highly of each other and chooses to see the good. Love doesn't shame others but instead points them to the grace of Jesus.

Love is not self-seeking. It puts the other person first and sacrifices its own desires time and again. It is stepping away from the entertainment the world brings to provide comfort and reassurance to the one person it pursues. Love lays down its own life.

Love is not easily angered. It remains gentle with words and actions. Love isn't drawn-out, cold silences nor is it piercing screams and broken dishes. It's choosing to still listen to the other person's thoughts and feelings, withholding judgment when those thoughts and feelings contradict its own. Love may get angry, but it doesn't stay that way nor does it make rash decisions based off that anger.

Love keeps no record of wrongs. It does not keep a list of sins committed against itself but instead runs to conflict for resolution and to introduce peace once again. Love forgives even when it seems impossible. Even when it is a long, drawn-out process. Love doesn't turn a blind eye to wrong, but it also does not keep reliving that wrong even after a resolution has been found.

Love does not delight in evil but rejoices with the truth. It does not cover up blindingly obvious character flaws but instead gently exposes them. It stands up for what is true and noble, what is right and pure, what is lovely and admirable, and whatever is excellent and praiseworthy. It seeks the uncomfortability of hard truth over the simpler path of easy acceptance.

Love always protects. It fights for what is worth being held on to. It pursues, chases, and captures even when the process is long and tiring. When outside forces threaten to shake the pillars of a relationship, love is the cement that keeps them standing strong. It is the shield that is held in front of the object of its affection, deflecting as much as possible the fiery arrows of a cruel world.

Love always trusts. It isn't fearing they will walk away or doubting your place in their life; it's trusting they will stay and knowing you are second priority to them with the first being their relationship with Jesus. It doesn't look into every spoken word and action in an attempt to find a flaw because you *just know this is too good to be true.* Instead, it works to conquer those fears and chooses to trust that they will always choose you.

Love always hopes. It encourages and feeds the beautiful dreams of a hopeful soul. It stands alongside its partner in all times of life. There is no fear because love casts it out. Love sees the injustices of a fallen world but chooses to hope that an imperfect replica of Jesus' love can be played out in this life in order to point others to Him.

Love always perseveres. When the weight of life pulls it down and the strong tides of the world push and pull it along, it keeps marching on. Marching toward unity. It doesn't only stay when it's easy and simple; it stays when it's unbelievably difficult. Loves pushes through despite any fears.

Love never fails. There are times it wavers and times when it is a choice, but it is always present. It always comes back stronger. Always grows. It never walks away into the still of the night, never to be seen again. Instead, it stays. It knows there will be times when mistakes are made, but it refuses to make a pattern of those mistakes. Love looks to the never-failing love of Jesus as an example and works to become more like His love every day.

Taking Back the Keys

I looked at the calendar on my phone to remind myself the time of an appointment I had coming up. I scrolled ahead a couple of weeks to find it. And I winced. Because my calendar is synced up with the national holiday calendar Google provides, I saw right there mocking and shouting up at me in dark green, *Valentine's Day.* Why on earth did my ex and I decide to have our first date the day before the country annually becomes inundated with roses and chocolates and cheesy, romantic gestures? It just made it way too easy to remember the first time we met each other. What had started off as an easy anniversary to remember became a cursed reminder of a chapter of my life I wanted to blot out. Like a cattle brand burned into my mind, the smoke still rose up to remind me of that mental tattoo, but the searing pain had finally turned into only a tender area. *Deep breaths in. Deep breaths out.*

The reminder of that day still stung. Images of the past still floated around in my head, but this time, they didn't haunt me. The ache of loss was still sometimes present, but I no longer missed him. While that day, once it finally rolled around, was difficult, it wasn't near as bad as what I thought it would be. Then the remaining days that I thought might bring some pain as well rolled around. And I barely noticed them. That once-familiar ache in my chest was no more. Tears no longer threatened to spill when a reminder of the past was brought up.

Over time, the grief of losing him turned into grief of losing a version of myself I would never get back. The hopeful girl who had started the previous year with a heart that had never been truly touched turned into a girl who was struggling to prevent her heart from hardening after barely piecing together its shattered pieces. The scars that accumulated changed how I viewed myself and the world around me and created a jaded perspective of life and love. One year seemed impossibly cruel. Depressing. Leaving me to wonder what was the point of even trying to heal. With that point of view, all I could see was the ugly wreckage, and all I could do was helplessly fall into despair that life won't be the same again. I won't be the same again. Only the past was visible with that narrowed vision. I could only feel the effects of an emotional hell instead of any good that may have come from it.

But then there's the flip side. The point of view that changes everything. The side of the story of my life that is the *truth*.

No, I won't be the same again, but I can see now that it's in a very good way. Once I broadened my line of sight and stopped gazing longingly into the past, I could see that the change I thought for the longest time would be a weight on my shoulders for the unforeseeable future was in reality a change that gave me life. Sure, I've left a version of myself in the past to be buried along with the hopes and dreams of a future spent with a man I had once loved. But that only opened me up to the possibility of becoming a better person. One who chases passionately after her Savior. One who still dreams big even if it now sometimes scares her. One who now does things that are uncomfortable because she knows there is growth found on the other side. One who still hopes for the love of the man God has for her but will still find joy even if that man doesn't exist.

Through it all, it allowed me to take back the keys to my heart I willingly gave away and instead hand them off to the One who would treasure it better than anyone else ever could.

About the Author

Melody Alcorn grew up in Tallahassee, Florida, and currently resides nearby where she works as a medical coding specialist. She has a passion for writing about her faith, and she can usually be found in a coffee shop putting her thoughts to paper. Melody enjoys spending quality time with her family and friends, serving in the children's ministry at her church, exploring beach towns, and relaxing with a novel in hand. *The Keys to My Heart* is Melody's first book.